The Hungry Heart

Also by Zoe Ann Nicholson

Matri, Letters from the Mother

The Passionate Heart

The Hungry Heart

Zoe Ann Nicholson

Lune Soleil Press

Newport Beach, California

The Hungry Heart

Published by
Lune Soleil Press
3419 Via Lido, Suite 614
Newport Beach, CA, 92663
www.lunesoleilpress.com

Art Direction & Cover
By Phillip Tommey

Principal cover photo
Courtesy Bloomington Pantagraph

May 27, 1982 Los Angeles Times
Article by Kathleen Hendrix
Copyright 1982, Los Angeles Times
Reprinted with permission
On pages 51 - 54

Printed & bound in
The United States of America

Library of Congress Control Number: 2004093618
ISBN 0-9723928-3-1

*This book and my fast
are dedicated to Mohandas K. Gandhi
and to everyone who uses
their life to experiment
with the truth.*

Introduction

Zoe Nicholson's *The Hungry Heart* is more than a moving personal account of the Women's Fast for Justice, an act of conscience by seven women who traveled to Illinois in 1982 to support ratification of the Equal Rights Amendment. Her words also provide a window into the US women's movement as it had evolved in the 1980's and reveal some of its many facets and factions from the inside. In her story we also catch a glimpse of the anti-feminist Stop ERA forces led by Phyllis Schlafly, the political descendents of the earlier anti-suffrage organizations that opposed votes for women in the early twentieth century.

Yet, *The Hungry Heart* is still more, much more, than one woman's account of dramatic historical events and movements. It takes its place alongside other works on the philosophy of non-violence - - memoirs of the British and U.S. suffrage movements, Mahatma Gandhi, Martin Luther King, Delores Huerta and Aung San Suu Kyi. Interestingly, Nicholson's reminiscences bring us full circle and reveal the woman's movement as the beginning and the end. The non-violent protests of the British suffrage women observed by Gandhi when in England inspired his campaign of civil disobedience in South Africa and, later, the practice of satyagraha in India. Gandhi's philosophy and actions, in turn, influenced King and the post World War II Civil Rights movement. And historian's agree that the movement to end racial segregation served as the model for the non-violent campaigns of every progressive cause which followed in the 1960's and 70's, including the Women's Fast for Justice.

Zoe Nicholson is a *satyagrahi*, just as Pankhurst, Gandhi, Rosa Parks, and Caesar Chavez were. Her clear and forthright exploration of her intentions and motivations invites us into the mind of those who create and follow the path of non-violent resistance to injustice

Finally, the memoir is an example of a long tradition of women's spiritual writings and teachings, documents of religious quest from Hildegard von Bingen, Julian of Norwich, and Teresa of Avila to such contemporary Buddhist and wiccan thinkers as Charlotte Joko Beck and Starhawk. For anyone interested in inner and cosmic journeys, *The Hungry Heart* is also an exploration of one woman's heart, soul and spirit struggles and joys.

As I read Nicholson's account of her weeks fasting in what Illinois residents immodestly call "the Heartland," I realized that readers unfamiliar with the political and historical context in which her story unfolds would benefit from a brief account of the Equal Rights Amendment and its history. Since I was a witness to the Fast for Justice, an Illinois citizen, and a participant in some of the events described, I can also provide some background and insight into the obstacles the ERA faced in Illinois.

The Equal Rights Amendment, first introduced in Congress in 1923, was an attempt to amend the U.S. Constitution to end sex discrimination in state and federal laws. In its original form it stated simply, "Men and women shall have equal rights throughout the United States and every place subject to its jurisdiction." The wording of the amendment changed over the years. It's final incarnation was consistent with two amendments, the 15th and 19th, granting the right to vote to African American men and to women and is stated in the negative: "Equality of rights under the law shall not be denied or abridged by the United States or by any state on account of sex."

After women won suffrage in 1920, the militant and more feminist wing of the suffrage movement, the National Women's Party lead by Alice Paul, turned its attention to ending all forms of legal inequality and discrimination. As in the earlier suffrage struggle, the NWP believed that a federal amendment would be the most efficient way to proceed. The organization drafted an amendment, had it introduced in both houses of Congress, and sought the support of other women's organizations.

Unfortunately, internal splits among suffragists over tactics during the campaign for the vote became a division over goals among women activists during the 1920's and 30's. For most of that period the NWP stood alone in advocating a federal equality amendment. The direct heirs to the mainstream

National American Woman Suffrage Association, the League of Women Voters, as well as many other women's organizations concerned with social justice, poverty and worker's rights, actively opposed the amendment. They feared that making the constitution and other laws gender neutral and treating men and women identically would actually harm women workers by negating hard-won legislation protecting them (e.g. laws setting maximum hours, prohibiting night work, regulating working conditions). It was not until 1937 that another large women's organization, the Business and Professional Women's Clubs endorsed the ERA and began to work for it.

The active opposition of powerful women's organizations and government agencies such as the League of Women Voters, the American Association of University Women, the National Women's Trade Union League, and the U.S Women's Bureau, as well as the declining power of the feminist movement in the 1920's and 1930's, prevented the ERA's passage by Congress. In addition, the NWP, its only active proponent, was a small and narrowly based organization of dedicated feminists. While it was introduced in every session of Congress from 1923 until final passage in 1972 and was frequently the subject of Judiciary Committee hearings in both houses, it did not get a favorable report out of committee until 1938. In 1940 the Republican Party included the amendment in its platform. This action, plus the economic concerns of the increasing numbers of women employed in industry during the war, gave the ERA new momentum.

Gradually, in the 1940's and 50's the amendment began to gain support, while still opposed by the powerful League of Women Voters, labor union women and others. In 1946 it was narrowly defeated by the Senate but was subsequently passed in that body in 1950. In the 1950's and 1960's the visibility and success of the Civil Rights movement also energized the women's movement creating what journalists and historians have called "the Second Wave." Another watershed event in the evolution of modern feminism and the pro-ERA movement was the 1963 publication of Betty Freidan's *The Feminine Mystique,* a work that raised awareness among countless women about sexism and inequality.

Government action also influenced attitudes toward the feminist goal of women's equality. The 1964 Civil Rights Act included "sex" as one of the classes covered by its anti-discrimination provisions. Presidential Executive Orders in 1965 and 1967 reinforced the act by applying its principles to federal employment and entities receiving federal contracts. As progressive ideas and goals became more and more popular in the 1960's and early 70's, support for the amendment broadened.

Sharon Whitney, in her book *The Equal Rights Amendment: The History and Movement*, argues that the modern campaign for the ERA, the push which resulted in its ultimate passage through Congress, began in 1967 when Alice Paul convinced the newly established National Organization for Women to endorse it. From that point on NOW replaced the NWP as the leader of the pro-ERA forces. It pushed for and won hearings before House and Senate committees in 1970. The measure was finally approved in the House of Representatives by 354 to 24 in 1971. The following year the Senate passed the amendment by 84 to 8 votes, but it also set the seven year time limit on ratification that was so problematic in the end. The overwhelming majorities for the amendment in both houses, far surpassing the 2/3rd vote required by the Constitution, encouraged many organizations to get behind the ERA. Even long-time opponent, the LWV, finally approved the amendment at its 1972 annual conference.

After approval of the amendment by Congress in 1972, it went to the 50 state legislatures for ratification. The approval of 38 states was required for the amendment to become law. Widespread support for the amendment and the progressive climate in the nation led to rapid approval in 30 states by the end of 1973; 3 more ratified in 1974 and another in 1975. Then, due to an economic recession and the growth of a more and more powerful conservative movement in the country, the amendment stalled. No state ratified in 1976 and only one, Indiana, in 1977, leaving the amendment with only 35 states having ratified, 3 short of the 38 needed. In addition, the 7-year ratification deadline added by the Senate was fast approaching.

The specter of defeat, after 55 years of struggle and near success, galvanized the feminist movement and its pro-ERA supporters. A NOW-led coalition of organizations including the LWV, American Association of University Women, Girl Scouts, Business and Professional Women's Clubs, Common Cause, both major political parties and a host of others formed ERAmerica in 1976 to coordinate efforts nationally. The first order of business was lobbying Congress and mobilizing public support for an extension of the time limit for ratification. The second was to educate the population to win even broader support and, at the same time, convince legislators in unratified states to vote for the amendment. A boycott of unratified states was one of several strategies designed to gain the three needed for passage of the measure.

After intense lobbying by representatives of the more than 450 organizations backing the ERA, Congress in October of 1978 approved the extension. A new deadline of June 30, 1982 was set. Although the proponents were gaining in strength, claimed 50 million supporters, raised millions of dollars, enlisted celebrities to the cause, and held mass rallies in some of the 15 states which had not yet approved, they also faced an increasingly active and well-funded anti-ERA movement. The proponents not only had the task of getting three more states to ratify but also had to fend off attempts by the antis in a dozen states to pass bills to rescind previous ratification bills. In a case that went to the Supreme Court, it was decided that states could not rescind their previous votes to ratify the amendment. The ERA boycott was also challenged in court by conservative opponents of ERA, but a federal judge declared it a legal tactic protected under the First Amendment, and the Supreme Court declined to hear an appeal.

By 1980, the opposing forces were involved in a bitter struggle over ERA in five states - - Illinois, Florida, North Carolina, Oklahoma and Virginia. Among the 15 states that had failed to pass the amendment, Illinois was the only large urban and industrial one. The battle here was especially intense and interesting because of several factors peculiar to the state. This peculiarity is one of the reasons that the Fasters, as they were called by journalists and by everyone who followed their story in the mass media, chose to come to Illinois. It is also why NOW and ERAmerica focused so much of their efforts, money and personnel on the Illinois legislature..

By all rights and reason, Illinois should have been in the ratification column for the ERA. By June of 1982, with the deadline looming, 67% of Illinois citizens supported the amendment. The vast majority of Democratic legislators and a few Republican senators and representative favored it; the Republican Governor, Jim Thompson, had also declared himself a proponent. Many churches, labor unions, civic organizations were also actively working for ratification. And the amendment had even passed each house of the legislature several times by a simple majority vote.

It wasn't right or reasonable, but Illinois failed to pass the amendment. This failure, and that of the other 14 states that did not ratify, meant that the ERA would not be added to the constitution. A part of the larger story of the struggle and ultimate defeat in Illinois is revealed in Nicholson's memoir. She laments the Illinois legislature's 3/5 rule, unique among all the states, for the passage of constitutional amendments. The rule required an undemocratic "super majority" of 60% for ratification. Ironically, the ERA received 60% support on votes in both the Illinois House and Senate, but not in the same legislative session. Nicholson also alludes to the relentless and well-organized campaign of Stop ERA, whose leader, Phyllis Schlafly, was an Illinois resident and focused much of her organizing talent and energy on her home state. The Hungry Heart reminds us, too, that Governor Thompson, while professing support for the amendment, did not support nor exert any influence on his party to change the undemocratic 3/5ths rule. And while Nicholson does not say so explicitly, she must have been aware that she and her sisters' courageous efforts were too little, too late. It is clear to some historians who have analyzed the amendment's failure, that it might have been successful if more women had fasted, committed acts of civil disobedience, and confronted recalcitrant state legislatures earlier, more consistently and in larger numbers.

One of the fasting women, Sister Maureen Fiedler, made a prophetic statement when the Fast ended on June 23, 1982. She predicted that "if the ERA does not pass now, we won't see it again, perhaps in this century." Sadly, she was right! A moment later she added, "We're not going to beg; we're not going to plead. We're not going to ask men for our rights any more. We are going to take them." I can only hope and pray that the example of the Fasters in Illinois in 1982, as well as the acts of defiance and civil disobedience by other women mentioned in this account, will inspire women to take their rights, to commit themselves to the feminist movement and to passage of the Equal Rights Amendment.

Mary Lee Sargent,
Bow, New Hampshire,
July, 2004

Acknowledgments

In 1982 the architecture and landscape of my life were women. Women in Newport Beach were my village: Maria, Jane, Sue, Laurel and Nancy. NOW was my fire. Dina was my beacon, lighting the way. The women in Illinois became my tribe: Sonia, Mary, Maureen, Mary Ann, Shirley, Mary Lee, Kathy, Judy, Vicki. Most especially my thoughts are with Judy Rosenfeld; her camera, her eye, her laughter, her point of view and her hard won wisdom, I miss them all.

In 2004 another tribe, one that travels digital highways, is close and loved. This book would not be in print if it were not for Patty, Phillip, Everett, David and Ann. Mary Lee gave me this introduction and it is a gift to all women. I am spoiled and grateful.

Foreword

I didn't need a purse. No cigarettes, no lighter, no money for snacks, no reason to carry a wallet. What I did need and worked to create for myself was privacy. I did it with a ridiculous red and white polka dot blank book.

When I could not cope, could not think, could not chat, could not laugh, could not cry another second; I wrote in my book. When someone came charging across the rotunda and I wanted to be alone, I opened my book and wrote something. When the news was so painful that I could not lift my face to offer a balanced response, I played with my pen and wrote. When the opponents chomped on candy and slurped their sodas, I removed myself by writing something, anything.

But most important, I used my blank book to ground me, to remember me, to protect me, to reflect on me. While we were all lonely and hungry, I had almost nothing else in common with the other fasters. I did not share sexual orientation, motherhood, religion or politics with anyone. I used my blank book to examine my motives, sort out my beliefs, search for my center, celebrate women and pray.

I imagine all of that shows.

Zoe Ann Nicholson
Newport Beach, CA.
August, 2004

Friday, May 14

This is something I want so much, I am willing to die for it. The fact that I want it for all women for all time makes it profound and suffocating. I feel like I am being crushed inside a storm of feelings, fears and certainty. I need some relief. I know this is the right thing to do. Food, cigarettes, privacy, pets, home and family -- take it. I want this more.

All I did was answer the phone. It sounded like every other ring that had called me to the phone. It rang in early May. It was Sonia Johnson calling. We had met in the Fall when she came to my bookstore to sign her book, "From Housewife to Heretic." We talked of the deadline for the Equal Rights Amendment, July 1, and promised one another that no matter what we did we would do it together. "We are going to fast for the ERA," Sonia calmly explained to me. "We are going to go to Illinois, sit in the Springfield rotunda, live on water only and win the ERA."

I met Dina at the Long Beach airport at 8 A.M. I think we are doing awfully well considering we both stopped smoking just four days ago. Maybe in the face of not eating, not smoking seems negligible. At least it seems to be just another task on my ToDo list. With an extra hour before the flight, we had breakfast. It was the first in the continuing series of meals we ate today. Eggs, Pancakes, Toast, O.J., Coffee. We ate as if there is no tomorrow.

The flight to Chicago was uneventful but we missed the connecting flight to Springfield. It took three attempts at stand-by to actually make it. The good news is that we were able to eat another meal; packing it away like chipmunks in Fall.

A thoughtful woman named Marion picked us up. She is studying to be a Methodist minister. She made the mistake of asking us if there was anything we wanted to do before we went to the meeting place. Fried Shrimp, Baked potatoes, Blue cheese salad, Pie, Coffee.

The mystery of where we are going to stay is solved. We have permission to stay at Kumler Methodist Church for two weeks. We are going to sleep on the floor of the Sunday School classrooms. The desks and chairs are itsy bitsy. The bathroom is down right comical as the sinks and toilets are all scaled down. The really bad news is that there are no showers. I am really taken back about no showers. It is muggy May in Southern Illinois.

The classrooms are stifling. I guess they only open the windows on Sunday mornings. The walls are covered with posters of Jesus. This is not the Jesus I love. This one is fair skinned, sandy hair, manicured hands, sweet little smile. The pictures show him surrounded with pastel covered, adoring fans. This is not the dissident, powerful, charismatic carpenter I would like to know.

Dina and I are the first to arrive. The other women are due in an hour or so. They are driving from D.C. and Virginia, where they have been stumping on the ERA trail. This is giving me too much time to sit and stew and get really scared. I can hear Dina in the next room; she must be recording her journal. I am stuffed but wonder what will happen if I don't have food for forty-four days. Maybe it won't take forty-four days. I'm hungry.

What if no one cares? What if there is no press coverage? If I was the opposition I would deflate this by ignoring it, trivializing it or even mocking it. But I have to remember that there is a magnificent precedent for fasting. Most of my favorite people have fasted. My heart says I have no choice.

I hear the others have arrived. Maybe they have some food.

Saturday, May 15

Seven women in a strange city. Seven women who will stop eating food in three days. Seven women who want to dress alike when appearing in public. Seven women who are different and yet there is a single focused intoxicating thrill in meeting one another, finding one another, celebrating one another. They want what I want. They want it as much as I do. I want what they want. I have never felt camaraderie like this before and I may never again.

The shopping list began with Sears and Penny's for whites. White shirts, white pants, white shoes. Washing machines have not been mentioned. Even without eating, we will need to do laundry on a regular basis. But convenience is not the criteria. The National Women's Party wore white. Suffragists wore white. We are going to wear white with purple sashes.

With bags of groceries, boxes of chocolates and soda cans, we headed back to the church basement. As dinner cooked, we took to our journals. The simple act of writing created seven private pockets like little individual domes around each of us. At last, over teriyaki chicken and white rice, we went around the table and shared why each of us is here.

Dina Bachelor amazes me, for all the years I've worked with her, I never knew much about her. She is a Pisces. She is forty and the only grandmother here. She is bursting with courage. She was a Jehovah's Witness minister for seven years. She has a degree in Business Administration and owns a retail store in L. A. She says she is ready for anything.

Mary Barnes is breathtaking. Just a few months ago she heard Sonia speak for the first time and here she is; a Mormon willing to confront her faith squarely no matter the consequences. Mary is the youngest in the group and has three young children. She is a Libra and, although she says that she is scared to death, I bet she will end up bringing balance to all of us. She is not tainted by movement politics and is here out of pure heart. I admire her because she says right out loud that she is afraid but has no choice in the matter -- fate simply made the decision for her.

How wonderful that Mary Ann Beall is as tall as I am. Now there are two Amazons. I really like this woman. She is a stone cutter. When Mary Ann was a child living in Europe, her mother apprenticed her to the town potter. She is a Quaker and a third generation feminist revolutionary. She said that we must become lighting rods called to act in faith. She is a Leo and her fire will ignite all of us. She has been performing acts of civil disobedience for many years, particularly during the Vietnam war. Her concern is how are we going to become real to the legislators so they don't just dismiss us as a side show. "I want to become real to those men."

I love Sonia. One look at her, at LAX where we first met, and all I saw was a sister. I believe that the Spirit of Woman lives in her heart, not the tiny steps forward made in the last two hundred years but the genuine agony of crushing oppression. Could she really be a Pisces? She is the most powerful speaker I have ever heard and, even in a kitchen with just six women, she speaks with inspiring resonance. She said that we must be pure in our attempt and not afraid. We must transcend our need to know results. Results must not be the issue here, only the purity of the fast.

Shirley Wallace is a Virgo. Ah, I am not alone. It's a good bet that once this group stops eating we will need double-dips of earth. She is a Mormon and, just as young Mormon men are expected to give a year of service to their church, she is giving a year of service to the ERA. She had a vision, which is not unheard of in Mormon circles (among men). She said that a female spirit embraced her and said, "Don't be afraid." She has four children and is from Colorado. I can't imagine having a mother like that! I hope her kids appreciate her.

The Scorpio in the group is Sister Maureen Fiedler. She is a Sister of Mercy. She is the president of Catholics Act for ERA and for the last four years she has lived in un-ratified states. I like her and I am fascinated watching her work so hard to reconcile her Christianity and her feminism which is radicalizing everyday. I suppose her beliefs on abortion must get in the way. She said she is afraid of the fast because she eats when she is anxious. Most of the weight she has gained in the last few years has been the ERA's fault.

We may be filling up on chicken but our hearts are bursting with the hope of changing history. None of our reasons are particularly reasonable. We seem to be here out of dream visions and irresistible compulsions. Everyone one of us is afraid but clearly have the courage to get this far. I feel as if we are pioneers. It sure isn't that society is calling us to do this. If this is a calling -- the call was made from far away.

I believe that each of us is listening to something celestial. I knew that I am on a spiritual quest but I had not expected it to be the case for the others. Leave it to me to be so self-centered as to think the heavens were talking exclusively to me as opposed to directing the fast in its entirety. NOW sees the Women's Movement as a civil rights movement but to me it is really a radical spiritual revolution. Woman Spirit is ready to make her move. Maybe this appears to be just a move on the men's game board but every woman who participants in this action will never be the same; ERA or no ERA.

The cigarette thing seems to be under control It has been six days on that front. I feel a bit spacey but the thoughtless lurching for a cigarette is passing. We bought several boxes of chocolates at Fanny Farmer today. It was as creamy and wonderful as I remember growing up and out in Wisconsin.

Sunday, May 16

Today I will become a satyagrahi. It is not that I am hoping to be a satyagrahi. It is not that one day I shall be a satyagrahi. Today I will be a satyagrahi. After all the years of reading and wishing, today I will become a satyagrahi. Today I will do what saints have done. I will do what Gandhi did. I will do what Alice Paul did. Today I will begin a fast.

It has been a long wait; one filled with focused study and faithful anticipation. Mostly it has been driven by love: love for the process, love for Gandhiji and love of the truth. Now I am going to become the truth. Before today I have tested the truth, but now I am going to give my truth physical form and I will be tested. I must pass. I must pass the test of the legislators, the test of society and the test of time. This truth will rise above censure. It will step outside of time. It will be pure and irresistible.

Am I asking too much of myself? It could be the case but I must go forward. My belief in social justice leaves me no alternative but to stand face to face with the opponents and force them to play their hand. My belief in feminism is simply the natural application of social justice. Today I will stand and refuse to cooperate with gender inequality. This is what has unfolded in my life.

Months ago a group of us met at Dina's house to discuss what to do in these last crucial days of the ERA campaign. We talked about what we would be willing to do. At the start everyone said that they wanted to do something significant. But, one by one, each suggestion was dismissed immediately by everyone except Dina and me. She and I were shocked. We could not believe this group of committed women said they didn't have the time. They didn't have the money. They didn't want to break any laws. To my mind, they didn't want to do anything. Last week, when Dina and I announced that it would be a fast and we were going, they told us we were crazy!

Is it really so crazy to be driven by one's beliefs? Is it crazy to physically express one's dearest beliefs? That is all it is really. Dina and I are offering to use ourselves to illustrate that it is time for gender equality to manifest on all planes of existence. Gender equality has always existed on the spiritual plane. Now it is time for it to exist on the physical plane. It is beliefs coming into form. We will be a living canvas, a sculpture.

Maybe it would be easier to practice satyagraha by choosing an oppressive law and publicly braking it but we have not been able to find one that uniquely demonstrates female oppression. It is an embedded part of our lives now. There isn't something to single out and say, "This is it. We draw the line here." Women can't walk out of their jobs to demand equal pay, equal insurance and equal social security. Women are already struggling with unjust economics. That would only hurt them more.

So today it is going to be a fast. It is active. It is spiritual. It is the way of the satyagrahi; fueled with love, formed by truth, spiritual in nature. The opponents will lose their footing as they find their spirits intoxicated with such a display of truth. They will be spellbound by its innocence and charmed by its grave dedication. We will change their minds because ultimately their spirits feel the truth and want it to prevail too.

The Hungry Heart

No matter what they say, no matter what they do, we must love them. We may have to love them through our own deaths, but that is the way of a satyagrahi. Our love will create an irresistible impression on even the most hardened of people. It will awaken them to what is right -- liberation. We are not just seeking the liberation of the oppressed, but that of the oppressors too. As the perpetrators, they are suffering more from this system than the oppressed. Breaking the cycle of injustice liberates us all.

What could be more simple? Today I will join six women to begin a fast. Today seven women will become the truth. We sit and wait and fast. As Hesse said about Siddartha; we will sit and wait and fast. So look out all you oppressors. Guard your hearts for today there are satyagrahis afoot. Without your permission or even your conscious participation, we are going to change your hearts about this system of yours. We are all going to be liberated soon.

Monday, May 17

PRESS RELEASE
Monday, MAY 17, 1982

Contacts: Maureen Fiedler RSM
              Jean Harvey

SEVEN WOMEN BEGIN FAST FOR THE EQUAL RIGHTS
AMENDMENT IN SPRINGFIELD, ILLINOIS.

On Tuesday, May 18, a group of women gathered in Springfield,
Illinois will begin a solemn fast for the ratification of the Equal
Rights Amendment. A press conference will be held in the Press
Room of the Capitol in Springfield at 10 A.M. on May 18 to
announce the fast and explain its purpose.

Seven women from around the country are beginning to
fast, including Sonia Johnson, the Mormon woman who was
excommunicated because of her advocacy of the Equal Rights
Amendment.

I think I just ate my last chocolate. I feel like I may
never eat chocolate again. We even demolished the box of
Fanny Farmer Milk Chocolates we bought for the church
housekeeper.

The Hungry Heart

It is just past midnight and I am fasting. There were no sirens, no bells or cheering crowds. But, as strong as the blackest velvety coffee, a reverence has poured over and through us. It feels like a surrender to an unknown who is making this choice for us. In fact, even though no one may get it, we believe that we are surrendering our bodies to the nation as a living sculpture to convey the gravity of women's inequality. I never imagined betting on anything this big and certainly not with my life.

This has been a very long day of non-stop working. I thought there would be all sorts of people here to help us. But it was only us; making banners, sewing sashes, writing press releases, phoning around the country, exploring any and all possible contacts. Just today I started to realize that Susan B. Anthony, Elizabeth Cady Stanton, Alice Paul were women like us. I had in my mind that they were queens with women crowding around them waiting for the next request. Now I understand they were only women who didn't wait for crowds of followers to collect. They simply collected themselves.

We all worked together in the big room near the pastor's offices. I sewed sashes and not very well either. I always rush through things. I wish I could just slow down and develop some patience. Mary Ann made two beautiful banners; E.R.A. EQUALS JUSTICE and WOMEN HUNGER FOR JUSTICE. Both say "DAY___" so we can change the number everyday.

In the midst of all these tasks, we made a thousand decisions: our purpose, our press line, our daily agenda, what we will wear, flyers, invitations, a stay on force feeding, directions for each of us in case of illness, etc. one major decision is that each woman will decide for herself as to how long she will fast. If one of us stops, it is her individual choice and has nothing to do with those who continue. If any of us is taken to a hospital emergency room, the ACLU has agreed to act on our behalf to see that a court does not order us to be force fed.

We worked on a flyer proclaiming every Wednesday from today through the deadline of June 30th, as a National Day of Fast and Prayer for Equal Rights. We are inviting everyone to participate with us in a way that works for them. First, they can come here and join us. Second, they can form fasts in their home town and tell their local press. As a bit of fun we have suggested, as they fast, they should send a paper plate to the Governor with a note about fasting for equal rights. We also hope they will wear purple armbands in solidarity.

Finally, we have asked people to hold fundraisers for the fast. I know this is necessary but I hate asking anyone for money. Friends and my NOW chapter bought my one way plane ticket. Since I didn't need any money for food, I just ignored the whole topic. Expenses are already adding up. Today we spent over a hundred dollars on the fabric for the banners and sashes. Not one of us planned how we are going to pay for any or all of this.

The press called today and said that they want to photograph our last meal. How silly and fun. We scrambled around the kitchen for over an hour to pull together dinner. There was enough food to feed the entire legislature of the great State of Illinois: chicken, pizza, peanut butter, a loaf of bread, potatoes and lots of soda. We were so embarrassed we didn't even bring out the ice cream. Before digging into our banquet we held hands and said a prayer for all women who have paved the way for us, those who would join us and those who will inherit whatever is won or lost here.

While there was fun and laughter on the surface, inside each of us knew that at midnight our lives would change forever. Deep down I feel I have finally found my place. I have discovered my link in the chain of women's history. I have always believed that I was born to live a life for more than just my own personal gain. I have always known that I would not have a family or be an artist. For thirty-four years I have tortured myself with one question, "What is my purpose?" I wanted to know why I was born. Now I know and this is my moment. So pass the chicken and take my picture, I have a purpose today. I am alive today.

Good night, Zoe. Tomorrow is just a wink away. Close your eyes and when you open them you will dress in purple and white and step into history.

Tuesday, May 18
Day 1

With the sun shining and the day full of promise the fast has begun. Up early we got dressed in our whites with purple sashes. We squeezed into two little cars and were on the way.

The Springfield Capitol looks like any other state Capitol in the U.S. The parking lot was packed with cars and not a human in sight. Probably everyone was already inside working at their desks. After landing two spaces, we locked the cars and walked unnoticed to the building, rode the elevator and opened the door to the press room. It was fantastic! People were jammed in like jelly beans, packed against the walls and into every corner. The press was there in full force: AP, UPI, NBC, ABC, CBS, CNN, NPR and all of the local papers. In the crowd there were contingencies from the Illinois Nurses Association, the AFL-CIO, the Illinois Religious Committee for the ERA and the former president of NOW, Wilma Scott Heide. There were so many I can't imagine who they all were. People were crying audibly. People wanted to shake our hands. People were acting as if they had been waiting as long as I had been preparing for this moment.

The press was mixed. There were several who were visibly moved and there were some who were openly disrespectful. One man was a real jerk shouting that we were absolutely ridiculous, which embarrassed others.

The Hungry Heart

Sonia stood at a podium and read our statement:

> We have gathered today in Springfield, Illinois to begin a solemn fast for the ratification of the Equal Rights Amendment. By making visible women's deprivation and by witnessing to women's deep hunger for justice, we seek to turn the hearts of the lawmakers to fulfill the Constitution's 200-year-old promise of equal justice under law.
>
> Fasting has been a part of momentous developments in this country. On May 28, 1774, Thomas Jefferson and other founding fathers inaugurated a fast "to implore a divine intervention to avert the destruction of our civil rights and to turn the hearts of king and parliament to moderation and justice." The fast, by unmasking the injustice of British rule, stirred the hearts of the colonists, led directly to a call for a Continental Congress, and made revolution inevitable.
>
> Two hundred years later, women are still struggling to gain our civil rights, and so today we begin our dialogue with the Governor and state legislators of Illinois: Governor Thompson, will you join with us in seeking democracy for the women of this nation by committing yourself to majority rule in the House and Senate? Mr. Speaker, will you open your heart and seek justice for us? Will you bring the rules change to a vote on the floor of the House?
>
> Does the State of Illinois have the courage to do the will of the American people who overwhelmingly desire the ratification of the Equal Rights Amendment?
>
> We have chosen to fast in Illinois because it poses the greatest challenge to ratification. This is true because it operates under the least democratic procedures of any state presently facing a decision about the Equal Rights Amendment. It has, despite all logic, insisted on a 3/5, rather than a majority, vote for ratification.

In this crisis in our country's history, when it seems -- unbelievably -- as if our Representatives are about to ignore our commitment as a nation to justice and democracy, and repudiate the American dream of equality, this fast is the most formidable call to conscience we know how to make. We hope the spiritual energy and enlightenment we generate will ultimately free both the oppressed and the oppressors from the cycle of injustice in which we have been bound.

We invite people throughout the United States to join us in the fast, either in their home states or in the Capitals of unratified states where the Equal Rights Amendment is under consideration. We invite the Governor and legislators of Illinois to join us in fasting to clarify their role in molding the destiny of this nation.

Perilous times in human history demand extraordinary focusing of spiritual power and love. These are perilous times for women. This fast is our act of love.

Then we all stood up and offered to answer questions. One reporter wanted to know why, since we were all from out of state, we had taken issue with Illinois politics. Although I wanted to tell him to call any eighth grade civics student, I actually told him that it was an amendment to the nation's Constitution and not state politics. They asked each and every one of us why we were there and why were we willing to fast for the ERA. My answer was that this is the first time I have been able to put my body and my heart in the same place with the same intensity.

From there we went to the Governor James R. Thompson's office. He agreed to see us. He is a very tall man and seems slick to me. He gave us the expected party line as he faces re-election in the Fall and the press was present. He said he was very sympathetic and in favor of equal rights, but he is not in favor of a rules change in the House.

The inner politics of Illinois' vote is particularly twisted and I am just starting to understand it. For any other bills on the floor, the requirement is a simply majority vote of fifty-percent plus one vote. They have been able to stonewall the Equal Rights Amendment by setting a higher standard of three-fifths. It would easily pass if it only needed fifty-percent plus one. Also Speaker George Ryan could hear a motion for a rules change but has flatly refused. He is creating an out for legislators to say they support the ERA but their hands are tied by the demands of the three-fifths rule.

We left the Governor and paraded out to the rotunda. It is a busy place, a cold marble hollow noisy place. High heels skid and wingtips squeak. For most it is a crossing station and never a destination. For us it is the center of the universe. We unrolled our banner and proudly stood next to it. We were proud of ourselves, proud of one another, proud of our ancestors and proud of our cause. The photographers were excited to have a new subject and the press was buzzing.

A state official came over to tell us we could not sit on the floor and that chairs are not allowed in the rotunda. We were informed that there is a fire law that forbids sitting. We may be feeling strong today, but this is going to become a major problem. Our commitment is to be in the rotunda every week day 10 A.M. to 2 P.M. until the ERA vote. Since this could last more than a month, it could mean wheelchairs or worse. Thankfully the Illinois Nurses Association came to our rescue and got clearance for seven folding chairs for exactly three hours each day. They also made arrangements for us to have our weight and blood pressure checked daily in the nurse's office on the third floor. We were directed to go there two at a time.

When it was my turn to go to the third floor, I found myself in the elevator with a dozen ladies dressed in red and white. I stood in the back and overheard them plot their wicked plan.

At exactly noon they would go to the rotunda newsstand, buy Snickers chocolate bars, march over to the fasters, unwrap the candy and eat them right in front of us. It wasn't funny enough that these women actually thought we would overthrow our dedication to equal rights for a Snickers. What was truly funny was that last night we gorged on four boxes of chocolates.

Up at the nurse's office the press crowded outside the glass door with full view of the scale. The cameras were posed to snap and document our weight. To gain control of this situation, one of us stood in front of the scale for the other. We have every intention to inform the press of our weight loss in one grand total, not individual amounts. The whole time I was on the third floor, I just wanted to get back to the rotunda for the Candy Bar Action.

Just as they had conspired, exactly at noon, the red and white ladies went to the newsstand and bought Snickers candy bars. They walked fifty feet, stood directly in front of us, unwrapped the bars and, with intent and passion, committed their political action. Aside from the irony of it all, it really made me wonder -- What are people going to think about this? What do people believe will deter us? The truth is nothing will deter us and the fact that they don't see it makes me feel lonely.

After the stint in the rotunda we went back to the church and had a few hours to ourselves. The actual church, in this maze of rooms and offices, is beautiful. It is all painted in high gloss white. I sat in a pew for a very long time and just stared. In front is an enormous cross, maybe fifteen feet tall. There is no body but rather a whip on one arm of the cross and a crown of thorns on the other. What on earth is that about? How could the congregation find it inspiring to see a whip wrapped in a circle dripping down from the cross bar?

Why do Christians want to think of their founder in agony and pain. Why not in triumph and glory? And why is the man in the classroom posters so wimpy? Are these people reading the same gospels that I studied? I read about a revolutionary Jew who was killed for his dissent. After teaching high school classes on the New Testament fourteen times, it is perfectly clear to me that he was a threat to all establishments, Jewish and Roman alike. Now he is being used to benchmark contemporary social behavior. Does the radical always dissolve into the conventional? Is it just a matter of time before the masses reduce a revolution and use it as a form of control? Once gender equality is the convention, will society find another group to oppress? I wonder who it will be.

I am tired, not hungry, just tired.

Wednesday, May 19
Day 2

Twenty-four hours ago I was in a sleeping bag on a classroom floor and here I am in the finest hotel in Chicago. Around noon today the people from *Chicago A.M.* called and invited two of us to be guests on the show tomorrow morning, all expenses paid. Sonia was the obvious choice. Since I was really excited about it, and the others just wanted to be left alone, I got to go too. We will be interviewed on air by Robb Weller.

We all went to the rotunda as the flight didn't leave until 3:55 P.M. This morning a doctor from Southern Illinois University came to the Capitol to warn us that fasting is dangerous. He mentioned Bobby Sands, from the Irish Republican Army, who died last summer after fasting for forty-five days. The press was writing down the doctor's every word. This is great for us, we want the public to be alarmed.

It was an unexpected blessing to get out of the rotunda today. The place was mayhem. Missing a meal can unravel the most patient and calm woman, but seven women not eating is trouble times seven. Everyone is teetering on a prickly emotional edge. Sensibilities are raw. Making matters worse, there was a jazz band playing within fifty feet of our chairs. Dina and Mary Ann were very upset about it and want to buy earplugs. No doubt the noise level is a serious consideration in trying to manage ourselves in the rotunda.

In my opinion, there was a strange energy in the rotunda today. It was pitchy and disorienting. At this point in the fast, maybe for the rest of the fast, we need to hold emotions on a tight leash. Much of the time I feel almost air-born like I am floating out of my body. Most likely all of us feel like we are losing our footing on planet earth. Sometimes it is pleasant but most of the time, especially when I need to concentrate, it is awful.

The flight to Chicago was scary through non-stop wind and rain. When the steward figured out who we were, he could not stop bringing water and doting on us. At O'Hare we hailed a cab and headed for the White Hall Hotel. The cab driver knew all about the fast. On the way he drove past Cabrini Green to show us where Mayor Jane Byrnes took up residence. He also showed us her other house on Chestnut Avenue. He told us that famous people stay at the White Hall Hotel all the time. Katherine Hepburn is there now and she jogs early every morning, leaving from the back door. When the Rolling Stones come to town they stay there too.

We checked in and the man at the desk clearly had no idea who we are. He said that the TV station was paying for everything so we could order freely from room service. I looked at Sonia and she looked at me -- all we could do was laugh. Oh my God, Carte Blanche! What a time for carte blanche. When we got to our room we ordered ice and ten bottles of Perrier.

I sent for an iron. I wanted to wash our whites, but there wasn't enough time. While Sonia took a bath I did what I do best in life -- iron. For women who haven't been near a bathtub for a week, a hot bath was much better than filet mignon or cheese cake. While each of us was in the bathroom, the other dialed up a storm phoning everyone back home. When it got dark we opened the drapes. The twinkly skyline, especially the illuminated Water Tower, was breathtaking.

Lying in our beds, talking into the night, our thoughts and feelings lifted like steam rising over boiling soup. We talked about our marriages. I told Sonia what a hard fall it had been for me as the myths of romance disintegrated one by one. Like Sonia's Mormonism, I had been a devout Catholic respectful of the sacrament of marriage. I married young and loved my husband. We were both idealists: marching for civil rights, opposing the Viet Nam war and fighting the draft. I wanted to be a school teacher and he was interested in prison reform. A couple of years after moving from Illinois to California, he felt cheated for having married so young. He was bored with our relationship and wanted to experience other women. Once I became aware of his many affairs, the marriage was over in a matter of months. I was broken-hearted. Our mutual dreams were gone forever. We both were sad. We lost the innocence we had celebrated together.

Then one day the entire illusion broke open for me. I am not certain why or how, but I realized that married life and parenthood were not my destiny. Being single was not a miserable life as a half person. For me it was a whole life, a complete life. This was not a lesson I could learn from school or from bride dolls under the Christmas tree. This is a rite of passage in a soul's unfolding journey. This is a knowing that is born out of pain, rejection and finally healing.

Thursday, May 20
Day 3

The alarm went off at 7:30. We are really out of gas. Thank goodness we don't need time for breakfast. I called Ruby and, as I had hoped, she said she would leave work to take us to the airport. We took a taxi to ABC. What a nightmare of a trip! We gave the driver the address. He drove, stopped the cab and said we are here. We got out and just stood there. We couldn't find it. Thinking that he let us off at the wrong place, we hailed a second cab. After this one pulled into traffic, we said, "ABC, Please." In fact we had been standing directly in front of ABC when he picked us up.

We waited in the green room. To my surprise, the room wasn't green at all. Everyone was nice, particularly Robb Weller. I didn't know where to look while he asked dozens of questions. Sonia answered most of them. Ruby arrived and waved while we were still on the air.

Once we got to the airport, Sonia wanted to sleep so we locked her in the car and headed off looking for postcards. I was really proud to be walking around the airport in my whites and sash. I have enlisted in the only army I believe in, fighting a just war for the liberation of women.

We went back to the car, collected Sonia and found our fight. 11A must be the tiniest commercial plane in the world. It had eight folding seats and when the pilot had something to say, he pulled back the curtain and said it directly to us. Since the plane was so small, it stayed low to the ground and, we could see the rich beautiful summertime farm fields of central Illinois.

While we were gone, there was an avalanche of phone calls. People all over the country are wearing purple armbands and some will fast on Wednesdays. The L.A. Times said that they are not going to print anything unless something terrible happens to one of us. 60 Minutes called requesting bios. And Dick Gregory is joining the fast -- not us -- the fast. I am not sure how I feel about this. I guess it will bring us some additional attention, but I prefer our group being women only.

Here is my favorite – it's a telegram --
Dear Zoe and Friends,
I'm awed by the risks inherent in what you have undertaken. If you call it off tomorrow you will have shown tremendous courage in the attempt. Please know how inspirational you have already been to women everywhere. And do call it off if your physical or mental health is endangered. We can't afford to lose such vital warriors in this battle. We'll need you for the rest of the war too.
With love, admiration and gratitude,
Peggy Kimball

This really is a battle, isn't it? There are lives at risk. The most endangered species on the planet is woman. What can women do after designing their lives to support marriage and children when their husbands move on for younger and childless women? What if a woman has no money of her own, no insurance, no pension, no social security? Women are battered, raped, held captive in economic slavery. I wonder how many women would stay with their husbands if they had good jobs and all the money they needed.

What is this battle? Who is the enemy? How can this injustice cover the entire earth? Why are some women fighting to maintain their secondary position? Am I trying to win something that people don't even want? It is very confusing, but I must do this. I truly believe that women must recover their power. Women must define their own lives and their place in society. Women must have absolute autonomy over their bodies and all reproductive decisions. We have to abolish gender categories in jobs, credit, education, property and contracts.

I want a world where men and women have equal opportunity to express themselves. I want sexism eliminated from the media and language and most of all in religion. I want women to define themselves and not be classified by marital status and ability to reproduce. It is a very simple premise: true justice is opportunity. All parties suffer when there is an imbalance.

The essence of Liberation Theology is that once one identifies who is the oppressed and who is the oppressor, it is one's obligation to join the oppressed; to work with and for the oppressed. The problems of the oppressed are my problems. The battles of the oppressed are my battles. This is simple justice, basic civil rights. It is obvious to me and I cannot be deterred from hoping to explain it or be understood.

Friday, May 21
Day 4

I am very hungry and I woke up very low. We had to get up an hour earlier than usual today because a reporter from the Bloomington Pantagraph is coming to interview and photograph us. I am not happy about it and neither are a few others.

We are on display for three hours a day in the Capitol and the only slice of privacy we have is here at the church. Even that barely counts as we are virtually never alone. Mornings are particularly unpredictable; physically and emotionally. We wake up to some great unknown in how our bodies are going to express the day's rebellion. Asleep you can forget all about it, but upon waking we become aware of what we are doing to ourselves and it is mostly unpleasant. We have found that it takes an hour or so to orient one's self to the unfed life. It is wobbly and unfriendly.

Moreover, I just want to be quiet. I mean deeply quiet. I don't want to open my mouth and I want to shut my ears. It feels fundamentally rude *and* that I am entitled to this rudeness. It is rampant because it is hard won, hard working, with hard edges. It is guilt free. But the fact remains that someone has agreed that a reporter will be here at 9 A.M. After a bit of a rhubarb, a) this man is coming, b) everyone should have been asked first and c) this will never happen again.

I think the reason this has grown out of proportion is that our energy is so limited. It isn't anything one could have prepared for in advance. The energy we do have has become guarded and precious. Resentments are easily provoked when anyone forgets that. Secondly, I believe that we have created a curious symbiosis that we can do anything as long as it is agreed upon. We are shoring up one another and won't let anyone fall.

To be honest, this part is really hard for me. I have never had to consult with six other people. Plus, I am accustomed to being around powerful, independent and willful women. I am used to being independent and willful myself. I think this must be true for all and each of us. It is not the big decisions either. It is a simple little thing like going to the bathroom or stepping away from the group. If I just want to drop a card in the mailbox across the rotunda, I have to tell someone where I am going. I know that is wise, but it is not something I have ever done before. We need to know each woman's whereabouts. Any harm coming to one of us would be a real undoing to all of us.

So Bernie arrived at 9 A.M. with his photographer unaware that his visit was a force majeure. And from his point of view, we must look like wilted wet noodles draping over our chairs. He was allowed in the work room, but not the classrooms where we sleep. At 10 A.M. we sat in a circle and meditated while pictures were taken. In our circle sit a Quaker, an ex-Jehovah Witness, three ex-Mormons, an ex-Catholic and a Catholic; silent prayer seems the obvious choice.

The chief offender at this point is our breath. It is putrid and offensive and unrelenting. It is our bodies throwing off toxins and from the smell of it, it could throw off Arnold Schwarzenegger. I am very embarrassed about it. It is just awful when a reporter leans in to ask an "intimate" question. One even went so far as to ask if we would have periods while fasting. I never thought of that. I plan to.

Rich Woods, from the Illinois Religious Committee for the ERA, called to tell us that Phyllis Schlafly is going to have two hundred pizzas delivered to the rotunda today at noon. Very Funny. When we arrived at the Capitol there was a lot of anxiety. Pizzas or not, the point was facing two hundred opponents in the rotunda. Whenever and wherever the Green & Whites (pro-ERA) meet the Red & Whites (anti-ERA), it is very distressing.

As noon came closer, dozens -- if not hundreds -- of people poured in from all of the surrounding office buildings. They formed a great deep circle insulating us from the Pizza Rebellion. It was a warm and loving gesture that fed us all. The pizza vendor never showed up. Later we found out that it was a joke that some columnist thought up.

Then from out of the crowd a young woman appeared with a gold florist box. She put the box on the floor and opened it. Inside were seven long stemmed white roses with a purple bow on each. Returning to the box seven times, one by one, she handed each of us a flower. She disappeared the very moment she finished. I don't know her name, but as long as I live I will never forget her. I hope someday she will know what a miracle she was for us that day.

Overall the reporters in the Capitol have been kind to us. It is certainly not what we expected after the initial press conference. The UPI and AP photographers just sit on the floor twenty feet away. Maybe they have nothing better to do. Several times a day groups of students walk past us snapping their cameras. When teachers are with them, they stop to explain what we are doing. It seems we are now figures in the current civics lessons.

Our weigh-in today shows that collectively we have lost fifty pounds. I have lost eight. It is scary that Sonia has lost the most as she has the least to lose. She began the fast at 122 and is now down to 113. She really isn't doing well. We are all feeling nauseous, but Sonia is particularly ill. Most of the day she is slumped on the lap of whoever is sitting next to her. This is only day four and I am worried about her.

A great woman from Washington D.C. has arrived, Dixie Johnson. She drove all the way with her car painted, "Illinois or Bust." She is a national NOW board member and a friend of Sonia's. Her energy is dazzling. She is ready for anything, springing into action with any request. She is an Aries and I love her.

The news is that Ellie Smeal is coming to town. I am anxious to meet her. I am curious about the leader of the largest women's organization in the U.S. The L.A. Times has finally broken down and is sending a reporter tomorrow for the duration.

I got my first shower tonight. Whew.

Saturday, May 22
Day 5

Dick Gregory arrived this morning. Although I am not
certain why he is here, at this point I am relieved. As much
as I care about the Equal Rights Amendment, he cares about
fasting and I think there is a lot we need to learn. Dina and I
went to the airport to pick him up. He will be staying at the
State House Hotel. We dropped him there, after making plans
to meet later.

Dixie took me to speak at a NOW meeting. It is a good thing
it is in the morning as I tend to tire easily and early. It feels
like there is a spigot in my leg and energy just pours out. It
happens quickly, without warning, and does not return for the
entire day.

The NOW meeting was at the First Presbyterian Church,
the church of President Lincoln. They have big rooms and
showers there. The Board of Directors is voting this week as
to whether or not we can stay here for the rest of the fast. The
heat is on at Kumler Methodist Church. Their board wants
us out and is voting Monday. I would love to be staying at the
church of Mr. Lincoln.

The NOW meeting was even better than singing to the
choir. What a cozy refuge. The women were visibly stirred and

generous. Comically, some of them were a bit embarrassed to be eating in front of me. I actually don't mind people eating around me. Don't mind the smells either. A few scrambled to hide their Fritos. I did stare big eyes at the cigarettes though.

There seems to be a mutual transfer of energy that occurs when I meet with people who find the fast inspiring. I become instantly rejuvenated and no longer hungry. They rekindle their commitment to the movement. It has been a slow and difficult struggle bringing the ERA vote this far. These local women have been working extra hard for an extra long time. I believe that standing here talking about the fast, the fasters and the plan feeds us all.

I love NOW. I think of NOW as the composite of a liberated woman. It is as if there is one grand soul of woman awaiting her entry through the hearts and intentions of the members of NOW. Maybe one day when there is no gender discrimination, each individual will be as powerful as the collective of NOW and NOW will not be needed. Just before I left the meeting, they took up a collection for the fast. That was a nice surprise.

This is turning out to be all I hoped it would be. Back in California I was terribly frustrated doing another bulk mailing or trying to put together another meeting. Here there are things to do and they have a real purpose. And the women! These women are spectacular. Dressed in green and white, they have come from all over the country and believe they are worth the fight. They have risked everything to be here. They have put aside their personal lives. They have prioritized and number one is Equal Rights under the law.

I wish I could bring all of the Orange County and Long Beach NOW women here. If they could see what is going on here, it would immediately stop any trivial bickering and frustration. If victory is not evident by June 6th, I think many of them will come here. They deserve to be a part of this.

Greg, as Dick Gregory has asked us to call him, arrived at

Kumler around 3 P.M. He is a refined and gentle man. I find him most pleasant to be around. He is not what I expected from a husband whose wife is home with ten children. While we are fasting on water, he is fasting solely on air. At one time he fasted on water for forty days while traveling to fifty-six cites in protest of the Viet Nam War.

He has traveled here because of his dedication to political fasts and fasters. He explained that he has personally dedicated himself to travel wherever people are fasting in the world; to be with them, help them, teach them.

He began by telling us that it is really important to ramp up to a fast methodically by systematically removing things from one's diet. I am certain he is not recommending twelve pounds of chocolates and teriyaki chicken. He went on to say that the first seven days are the toughest because the body is trying to adjust and is throwing off the toxins we have spent a lifetime accumulating. His biggest shock was all of the stairs we climb everyday. He said that we should be lying down and conserving energy.

As time goes on we will become less and less grounded. Greg said that we could get so far out of our bodies, we may not be able to get back. There may be a type of depression, or inner sadness, when we start eating again because we will be losing the purity we have found through fasting. "Fasting is really a method of curing," he said. It is meant to heal. It is exactly what our pets already know. When my cat or dog feels sick, they hide under the bed and fast until they feel better. Our bodies will become dormant. Everyday we fast we will not age because the aging process is caused by digestion. Our bodies will be sleeping and our consciousness will be heightened. Awareness will become the primary sense.

One reason why fasting is successful and impressive is that everyone in the world knows how it feels to be hungry. "When eaters eat, they will think of us." He told us that right now the universe is smiling on us. We are living the purist moments one can live. These are moments of total dedication and intent. I feel that. This is the only time in my life when I am not doing anything meaningless or useless. Every second of the day I am living my beliefs.

Finally, Greg wanted to emphasize that how we end the fast is very serious and very important. Waking up the body is dangerous and requires vigilance. The first day it should be nothing but grape juice diluted with water in very small increments, maybe two ounces every thirty minutes. The second day it can expand to a strained mixture of eight lemons, a gallon of water and a cup of honey. The third day one can have salt-free V-8 juice heated and eaten with a spoon. The fourth day, a compote of dried fruit and honey that has been soaked in water for twenty-four hours. He warned to not eat cooked food for at least three weeks. I am confident in saying that, no matter my condition, I am going to have oatmeal, raisin toast, a club sandwich, coke, ice cream and SNICKERS!

Sunday, May 23
Day 6

Today is Sunday and that means that we had to get out of the classrooms early and without a trace. We went to the State House Hotel to meet Kathy Hendrix, the reporter from the L.A. Times. We piled into her room and took turns taking showers and baths. She said that the Times had given her an expense account for taking interviewees to dinner and asked if there was anything in particular she could buy for us. Much to my humiliation what we needed, according to Greg, was enema bags.

I assured everyone that I would not need one. I have no intention of doing *that* for me or the ERA. But Greg had gone to great lengths to explain that poisons will be collecting and need to be escorted out. Since they will evacuate one way or another, it is important to take control of which orifice they use. I have not told anyone yet, but I am already having trouble with my vision. I can write for a few minutes and then everything goes blurry. It lasts for five to thirty minutes and then clears up entirely. I know that the Irish fasters went blind, but Greg said it was because they drank tap water and took salt tablets.

As of Greg's arrival, we are drinking spring water only. We were lavishing in Perrier until he blew a gasket about it. He said that the salt was lethal. Sonia and Dina are feeling very bad and there is speculation that it is their kidneys. We have been advised to drink a gallon of water everyday, but I know I can't possibly choke down a gallon of water a day.

Dr. David Spencer, chief of Southern Illinois University School of Medicine Family Practice Center, has offered to see us for free and monitor our electrolytes. None of us feel right about that choice. We cannot disregard the fact that Dr. Spencer is funded by the great State of Illinois. We could never be entirely certain of an unbiased opinion. Who can say if this fast might escalate into something controversial and the Governor might want to taint it in some way. All they would have to do is report that the urine or blood work indicates that we are eating. Right now, the fast is obvious as none of us is looking very good.

Dina, Mary Barnes and I have no confidence in traditional medicine at all. Besides, there is a lot of information reporting that fasting is healthy and wholesome. We arrived here with twenty books between us on fasting. Author Paul Bragg highly recommends it. Basically I brought two types of books; those that say you must use an enema and those that do not. I am counting on the second group and expect my vision to clear up tomorrow.

Tonight was our first publicized open prayer meeting. It was held at Kumler Church, 7 P.M. There were many people, maybe thirty. I never expected organized religion to be a component in this, but they are really coming to our aid. Catholics for the ERA and the Illinois Religious Committee are arranging almost everything for us. I had expected that there would be rituals, candles and talk of the Goddess. Probably the public would disapprove of that and would feel excluded. Maybe this is much better.

Greg spoke at the service and said that in the world there are two primary things going on. One is the Falklands and the other is the fast. In the Falklands it is men working out their differences with guns and here it is a solemn fast for human rights. He went on to say that if God was incarnate today, he would choose to be with us.

Monday, May 24
Day 7

Today is a nightmare. I feel helpless and lost. I can do almost nothing by myself and have to wait for help. I am trying my very best to not let it show but I feel like butter in a red hot frying pan; sputtering and ultimately evaporating. I want to cry every five minutes.

We went by the hotel and picked up Greg. The press was giddy over this new celebrity to fawn over. Any concern we had about him joining us has vanished. He has demonstrated again and again that he is here to spotlight the fast, the issue is equal rights and he is honored to be here with us. Over the last week, we unintentionally started sitting in specific order. Since I am on the open end, Greg is sitting next to me.

Sonia is entirely wiped out. The folding chair is not holding her up and she is lying on Shirley's lap. Dina looks her beautiful self, but she is using her usual make-up. If you look through it, you can see she is really suffering. Maureen and Mary Ann are upstairs most of the time, knocking on doors to lobby members of the House and Senate. My vision is completely unreliable. Everything is blurry. I start to cross the Capitol floor and I just freeze, afraid to take another step. I can't count on myself for the simplest of things. Dixie walks with me to the bathroom and mailbox, but that leaves the others alone.

Now a conflict has broken out in the ladies room. It seems that the attendant is outraged with the fast. When one of us is in there alone, she sprays disinfectant all around the stall that we are using. It is asphyxiating and intensified by fasting. We were not certain of her intentions until she came over to us and yelled full force that we are ridiculous and should stop immediately. She is angry and looks so unhappy. I feel as if she is ashamed of us. She is embarrassed that we are fasting for her rights as if she isn't worth it. I want her to know that she is worth it and we are not a joke.

Once we settled in and the press finished their daily interrogations, Dina (on my left) and I began grilling Greg about what is actually happening to us. Of all of us, we are the most interested in the metaphysical aspects of fasting. We both feel certain that there is something otherworldly going on, something invisible but perceptible. We want to know everything about fasting: history, effects, dangers, successes. Why do people begin interior journeys with fasting?

Greg said that we are going to put our bodies aside for a while and, for the first time, we are actually going to be able to feel our true selves. Since our cells will no long be clogged by everything we have accumulated since birth, we will be able to feel our natural vibration. We will feel our very souls. We will achieve a new level of consciousness and we will be able to remember it. Remembering its stillness, its refinement, is so powerful and prayerful, eating again will be painful. Knowing what we will be giving up by eating, we will grieve.

Greg went on to tell us that, in a matter of days, we will be able to feel a Divine Presence. It is like sitting in a room and a little mouse cautiously comes out of the woodwork. If you stamp your feet, the mouse will run away. Divine Presence stays in the room until a person exerts their will. When fasting, everything slows down, feet stamping stops. You are able to rest your will and God comes forward. Eaters believe that they are in control and are acting independently. Fasting makes that illusion drop away. It will become clear that we always rely on God and are living in God's grace. Every move, every thought, even thoughts of independence are dependent on God.

During a long term fast, such as this one, we are lifted into a very delicate state. Greg said that we should be lying down and the press should be coming to us. We should be extra cautious to not strain any muscles. We should not be carrying anything heavy because nothing can be done for a muscle pulled while fasting. Oddly, he said that when people fast, the weather is always cold and rainy. That has proven true for us. It had been sunny and muggy, but now it is dreary and drizzling.

After the three hour stint in the rotunda, Dina and I went to the mall with Kathy Hendrix. Since laundry is a big problem, we need additional white tops. While roaming around the stores Dina got really nauseous, so she and Kathy went back to the car. They said they would pick me up in front of Wards in ten minutes.

Right on time I went to the door and they were nowhere in sight. I sat down on the curb and waited for thirty-five minutes. I started to panic. I lost faith in my hearing and thought maybe they said Sears. I walked the entire length of the mall to the Sears end. Still, no one in sight. No one at the door on the other side of Sears either. An hour passed and there I was alone in Sears with my vision going in and out of focus. I asked a clerk to help me with a phone and called a cab.

No cab came. I found the furniture department in Sears, sat on a couch and started to shake. My mind was in a wild fritz. What is happening? Why did they leave me? Why aren't they looking for me? What will I do? I collected myself just long enough to call the cab company again. Finally one arrived.

I slumped into the back seat and trembled all the way to
the church. As I was struggling to get out of the car, Greg and
his brother spotted me from across the street. They ran to me.
They consoled me. They told me I should have expected to be
disoriented. It will be easy to get lost. None of us should be
out shopping and never alone. Inside I found Dina and Kathy
frantically calling the mall, asking them to page me. They had
waited outside of Wards for forty-five minutes and figured that
I must have called a cab and left.

Besides that catastrophe, the church board voted a flat no
and we must be out of Kumler Methodist Church tomorrow.
The Unitarian Church has also said no. The only option we
have at this time is an attorney who has offered her home. It is
a split level with two showers and three bedrooms. Tomorrow
morning when we go to the Capitol, we will not be returning to
Kumler. Some NOW women will come and collect our things.

Tuesday, May 25
Day 8

Sonia is in wheelchair. This is only day eight. If they don't ratify before the deadline, there are thirty-seven days left to go in the process. Although it is an individual decision, I really do believe that not one of us will choose to eat before the deadline. I am feeling pretty good but shaky. I can only guess what the effects have been from sleeping on wood floors and occasional showers. In front of the press there is an air of hope and expectancy but here, in the inner circle, we are becoming profoundly quiet and withdrawn.

The high soaring woman spirit that sewed and marched a week ago is already in hibernation. In the rotunda, when everybody is staring at us, we appear to be lit up, but when no one is looking the light switch is definitely off. I think part of the electrical charge is the public's expectation. They carry a spark. Now that flash of excitement and energy is almost painful and we are trying to insolate ourselves through silence and emotional distance.

The house where we are staying is okay. It has showers and that is fantastic. Bathing is not vanity but necessity now that we are sloughing toxins. I also believe that we need to shower off a lot of the negativity that is thrown our way sitting in the Capitol. However none of us was prepared for the kitchen. It has been eight days since we were near a kitchen. It has salt and pepper shakers. It has a refrigerator. None of us would ever even touch it, let alone open it. There is cereal and canned chili. There is sugar and coffee. The house phone is in this room of earthly delights. We have to talk with eyes shut.

I spent over two hours phoning today trying to locate a hotel that has six double occupancy rooms available for six weeks. While the expense seems monumental, the big obstacle is that none have rooms for six weeks straight.

Dixie found rooms! The Ramada Inn has everything and we are moving there in two days. Sheets, showers, TVs, phones, a double bed for each, two to a room. Paradise.

The media is on the move. Tomorrow we will be on the Today Show. All of us know that Dick Gregory had a lot to do with that. He had been scheduled to be on and intentionally arranged to be in Springfield with us. He worked it so they would interview him here and include the fast. A reporter from *Time* magazine has arrived, although I don't know who it is. *People* magazine has called and is sending someone to spend four days with us at the Ramada Inn. Kathy Hendrix's article in the L.A. Times will be out this week.

We are the lead story on the local TV stations. We sit and watch and appear glib. I am not. I am deeply moved. I know I am romantic and idealistic, but I have never been a principle in a drama before. I might see a movie or read a book and feel as if I know the characters, understand their journey, love them, care for them. Now I am the one in the story and I am just as moved. I am marching on line with Alice Paul. I am sitting with Rosa Parks. I am resisting with Gandhiji. I have put down my books and am walking with Oscar Romero. I am writing and working with Dorothy Day.

And in the midst of this nostalgia and devotion, what I am really discovering is that we are all just people. We are human beings who are not satisfied with things as they are. We see that there could be more. There should be more. What we all have in common is that we are all hungry for more.

I am just as confused as ever about why there are so few of us. I consider the longing for liberation and justice to be obvious and ordinary. People tell me that they could never do this. Sure they could.

Wednesday, May 26
Day 9

The rotunda carnival was the same today with lots of crazy-making people and all the little fasters all in a row. For some reason, or no reason, we have been sitting in the exact same order every day. I am the last on the left which puts the elevator to my right. Throngs of people pour past me, most of them with food and drinks. We have placed ourselves precisely where and when people are on a mission for their lunch. I can smell it all, right down to the dill pickles.

And so we sit. The crowds buzz around us with their opinions and judgments, always just loud enough for us to hear clearly. They seem to be in two distinct groups. They hate us and think we are actually mad and wicked or they think we are sainted. Neither of them is true which leaves me feeling isolated and sad. It isn't that I want them to know who I really am, but I want them to know that we are women, ordinary women. We are their sisters, aunts, mothers, wives, teachers, nurses, neighbors who are unrecognized and disregarded first class citizens. We are the seven who are here and the rest of us, the millions of us, are at work in factories, in hospitals, in schools and homes all over this country. Many women in America will make and eat dinner tonight because if they don't, they will put themselves and their children in danger.

The Hungry Heart

Greg sat with us all day. He seems peaceful and resigned. He always has a paperback book in his back pocket. I have tried several times to see what it is. Tonight, sitting in the living room of the loaned house, I asked him what authors he likes. Emmet Fox. Charles Filmore. Joel S. Goldsmith. I knew that he had to be reading something interesting. His depth is far beyond a person who only wants agreement and flat, easily digested answers. Every now and then he says something poetic and profound. Today he said, "You can plant the seed but you can't control the crop. It's not your sun. It's not your water."

Once again Greg tells us that fasting is more spiritual than political. He maintains that fasting can only occur on the side of the spirit. It is a pure act and is never used for impure motives. As he asks, "Can you imagine fasting in favor of slavery?"

He has also talked a great deal about the curative properties of fasting. He believes that buried deep within the cells of a human body are seeds of every illness one will have during their lifetime. These sit in a dormant state and awaken, triggered throughout the years by various circumstances. When one fasts, a sleeping and stored illness will surface and express. Whatever has been repressed through pharmaceuticals rises to the surface to be flushed out. He even goes so far as to say that we will be able to trace our physical development chronologically by watching what we are going through.

In other words, he is saying that our physical history is buried within us, like rings in a tree. When fasting we will recapitulate our medical biography. If one had pneumonia at age five and it was not fully expunged, the stored symptoms will manifest because of and during a fast. It is not to be feared, but fostered and managed. It is why fasting is thought to be purifying. The expression may last a day, an hour, an evening. It is transitory and ultimately beneficial. Should any of us excavate a dangerous or frightening mine of illness,

Greg has given us the name and phone number of a woman in Chicago who will pray for us.

In my heart, I am far more interested in her prayers. Why are her prayers effective? Why are anyone's prayers successful? Who are they praying to? Is there someone somewhere receiving prayer? Candles, chanting, angels, rosaries? What is all this about? Is it knowable? Is the longing important, the depth of longing, the duration of longing? Is it related to the purity of the petitioner? Or the intent of a particular prayer?

Bernadette, Theresa and Francis have led us to consider that prayer is a functional tool in spiritual growth. They seem to tell us that there are certain words to be said, at a certain time, in a certain place. Millions of people spend time everyday praising God or pleading their case. To be truthful, I don't see results from it. I am much more drawn to believing that one's life is one's prayer. How I treat people is my prayer. Fasting is my prayer. I am praying for women and my fast is my prayer.

Thursday, May 27
Day 10

Miracles 136, 141, 143, 145, 147 + 149. Crisp sheets, white towels, double beds, shower, tub, telephone, TV, wake-up calls, swimming pool, summer grass outside the door, corn fields across the yard. While I did not expect heaven to have green striped wall paper and gold velveteen bedspreads, this is paradise. Sleeping bags are packed away and I am going to take at least two showers every day.

Dina and I are sharing a first floor room at the end of the main building. Across the path, the rest of our rooms are all in a row. Mary is in a room by herself for a couple of days, waiting for my friend, Judy Rosenfeld to arrive on the 5th. Mary Ann and a new faster, Mary Woods (Woody), are next. Then come Shirley, Maureen, Sonia and Dixie. After the three hour exhibition in the rotunda, we drove here and found all of our gear in the right rooms waiting for us.

At this very moment I am watching an episode of, "I Married Joan." What a Girl. What a Pearl. What a Wife! It is not a feminist show, but I need to laugh. TV in central Illinois has ads for tractors and feed stores. The Dairy Queen commercial just may be our undoing with mountains of soft ice cream and rivers of hot fudge. And although I have never eaten one in my life, I now want an Egg McMuffin.

The evening news always opens with us. We are the lead-in story every night on the local channels and most nights out of Chicago. After seeing us on TV, Dina is beside herself about her hair. I look fat. I don't feel fat, but I look fat. Sonia looks like her life force has drained out almost entirely. She is pale and weak and thin and chilling.

Dixie is a pogo stick. She wants us to have everything we could possibly think of and she wants us to have it the very instant we think of it. Kate, a new arrival, has volunteered to help her. She doesn't know any of us. She heard Sonia speak and told her family that they would have to make do without her as long as the fast lasts. She is rooming with Maureen. Another woman, who lives in Springfield, has offered to do our wash every night, returning it in the morning. So it appears that this is all coming together and it is not a minute too soon. There is no energy to spare, to lavish, to feign.

When we arrived at the rotunda today, four women from the NOW office came over to us and said that they are officially assigned to guard us. Louise, Judy, Kathy and Vicki are dressed in green and white and seem happy with this new assignment. Part of me, the Catholic-raised, self- effacing, guilt-ridden woman, feels embarrassed with this amount of attention, all this fanfare. But in my heart I know this is right. Regardless of me being one of them, the seven women who are offering their lives for equal rights deserve this and so much more.

The fact is we need to consider safety and possibly needing guards. The crowds are growing and hostility is boiling up and spilling over. The entire atmosphere is thick with fear, hope, mockery, a wide buffet of emotions. With the passing of each day, we are becoming removed and less human to everyone. Some people stand just a few feet away and talk about us as if we have no ears, no feelings, no rights. They push and shove and don't respect our space. They step on our feet and bang into us. Yesterday a man intentionally jammed his lit cigarette into my arm as he passed by. I am sad about that. And even the people who support us have lost perspective. They think we are superhuman which removes us from their immediate family. That seems sad too.

NOW's gift of security and safety is a semi-circle of love standing around us in the rotunda: Louise, Judy, Kathy and Vicki. They keep everyone a few feet away. We can breath a bit, relax a tiny bit. We don't have to be on alert, which is so exhausting. They let in the press. They let in friends. They are concerned and brilliantly efficient. It is how I remember being when I was eating. I remember being capable and organized. Now I just want to be quiet and insulated. I feel fragile and extra touchy. Do they know I am a leader? Do they know that I am smart? Do they know that I am well read and clever? I feel like a shell of a woman sitting silently in my chair, holding a glass that magically fills with water the instant I look away.

I am just a helpless child now. I can't walk to the mail chute by myself. I can't even go to the bathroom by myself. I can't walk alone across the rotunda anymore as my vision is almost always blurry now. So tonight I did the unthinkable; the BIG E, as we have come to call it in public. I swore I would not do a big E, but the vision thing is really scaring me. Not being able to read and, eventually, not being able to write is more than I can endure.

Friday, May 28
Day 11

The LA Times has run a huge article today. Here are a few sections --

Women Fasting for ERA and Hungering for Justice
Religious Zeal Sustains Illinois Demonstrators
By Kathleen Hendrix
Times Staff Writer

Springfield, Ill – So finally, it has come down to this – a handful of women, most of them mothers, fasting on water, sitting in the rotunda of the Illinois Statehouse, growing visibly weaker by the day, hoping somehow to move the legislators and the people of America to make the equal-rights amendment part of the Constitution before the time to ratify runs out June 30.

Today will be the 10th day of this "solemn fast of indefinite duration" for this small group that Sonia Johnson, excommunicated from the Mormon Church in 1979 for her support of the ERA, has brought together.

Johnson is already using a wheelchair. She is 46, the mother of four children and a slight figure. By late Monday, day seven, her weight had dropped from 122 to 110 pounds. She can still walk, but has to be helped rising and taking stairs, needs support if she is going to take more than a few steps and finds it next to impossible to sit upright for any length of time on the hard metal folding chairs in the rotunda.

The Hungry Heart

Usually a lighthearted woman with a playful sense of humor and a "gosh-darn," "gee-whiz" quality to her speech, she remains, for all her physical weakness, in good spirits and is the comedian in the group. She is dead serious about the ERA and the fast, however, and will drop all wistful jokes about Big Macs and eggs-over-easy to explain what she is doing.

"We're trying to symbolize women's suffering," she says. "Nobody sees women's pain. We suffer for all those women out there. We're representing them."

Another of the women, Sister Maureen Fiedler, a Catholic Sister of Mercy and national coordinator for Catholics for ERA, distinguishes between a hunger strike and a fast. Theirs is not a hunger strike, not a protest.

"This is an attempt," she said, "to bring together whatever spiritual energy we can to focus on this problem. "

The problem, getting the ERA ratified by three more states by June 30, is one that will require enough spiritual energy to work a miracle. The women know that and seem undaunted.

This is a deeply spiritual group. They refer to their spirituality, their religious roots, their Christianity frequently and say it is this dimension to their feminism that bonds them and is motivating them.

The fasting women have chosen Illinois out of all the unratified states to keep their vigil, they say, because it is the land of Lincoln, because it is the only northern industrialized state that has not ratified, and because it is the most difficult.

Five of the women are mothers, and to the concerned, sometimes righteous-sounding questions raised about their responsibilities to their children – leaving them, endangering their own health, maybe risking death, they answer sharply, "Who do you think we are doing this for?"

Dina Bachelor, who reared four children on her own, sees the ERA in economic terms, and she smarts when she talks about the necessity for it, and for her action, using her own life as an example. Working since she was 13 and nothing to show for it; earning half as much as men doing the same job; seeing herself replaced by two men once, both hired at higher salaries than hers. She docs not want her three daughters to have to repeat that.

How Far Will They Go?

"That's a cop out," Sonia Johnson said of using children as an excuse not to act. "Parents are supposed to be making the world a better place for their children."

They will not say how far they will go with this fast. At times they have indicated they will fast either until the ERA is ratified or until June 30. Would they fast beyond June 30 if the ERA goes down? Would they die for this?

They are not saying and it seems they have not answered these questions for themselves. They say they will have to be answered individually when the time comes.

Continue....

The Rotunda

The hours in the Capitol seem to be both rewarding and trying for them. They sit dressed in white under a purple and gold banner, saying, "Women Hunger for Justice" a few feet away from a huge bronze statue of a woman, arms outstretched, its base engraved, "Illinois Welcoming the World. Commemorating the Work of the Women of the State of Illinois at the World's Columbian Exposition 1893."

The rotunda is a steady stream of schoolchildren, foreign tourists with cameras, legislators, lobbyists, aides and staff. Most stop to at least stare...

One cleaning woman at the Capitol seems to have become fixated on the fasters. She is very angry, and she cannot stay away from them. She crosses the rotunda constantly, glaring at them, then deliberately feigning no attention, her face frozen in disgust... She hung around a corner one afternoon, holding a trash bag, leaning on a banister out of sight, watching a woman helping Sonia Johnson into the restroom.

What did she think of it?

"I think it is dumb."

And the ERA itself?

"I think the whole thing is dumb. Women ought to stay where they belong. They can't live in a man's world. There is no way they can go out and work on a bridge construction crew. And they still want men to open doors for them."

For the most part, the women say the experience is positive. They have been receiving a lot of support from local women. The NOW chapter passed the hat at a meeting and collected $1,000 for them. NOW workers, in town to prepare for a massive rally on June 6 in support of the ERA, have been encouraging them, attending prayer services with them, lining up practical help for them – such as bringing chairs to the Capitol every day.

Just a few feet away from the fasters in the rotunda, representatives from the League of Women Voters come everyday to stand with their banners and keep vigil for the ERA, just as they have everyday the legislature been in session for the past 10 years.

"I dropped my sign a few minutes ago," Marjorie Chapin from the Springfield chapter said, "and a No Vote (senator) helped me pick it up. He said he hoped no one took his picture. I asked him why he voted no and he said, whenever he polled his district...."

How does it make her feel after 10 years?

"Tired. It's a shame we have to go through all of this," she said, nodding at the fasters, "just to get equality put into the Constitution."

'Separation of Powers'

No one expects the governor to step in to change the three-fifths rule. His office talks of, "separation of powers" and how his hands are tied. Moreover, he has said, and told the women, that is an important rule. Rather, his press aide David Fields said, he has announced his time will be better spent trying to influence the legislators to change their vote. So far he has announced one such change. For the most part he has put the burden back on ERA supporters, advising them to contact their legislators.

Zoe Ananda* sat in the rotunda, looking inward yet again, to explain why she was there, why it is so important to her.

She knows the ERA will not put an end to all of the injustice she sees around her, she said. It will be no cure all. There will be plenty of court fights.

She is certain, however, that if it does not pass, much will be lost. She would rather talk about its passage. The ERA will be, at least, an opening for equality, she said. And so she will fast for it.

"I am ready to go the distance," she said. "I feel there is plenty of hope. That's what I want to get across to women. There's plenty of hope. Come on. We expect a miracle. Let's get out here and go to work."

*Ananda was my last name for several years. I chose it because it means joy.

54

Saturday, May 29
Day 12

Today nothing is scheduled. Oh happy day. I got up at 10 A.M. and went back to sleep from noon to 5 P.M.. It is now 8:30 and I am still exhausted. It is fantastic that there is nothing on the schedule for tomorrow either, but Monday may be one of the best days in my life. We are going to spend Memorial day at Mr. Lincoln's tomb with Dr. Joseph Lowery, the current President of the Southern Christian Leadership Conference. I am going to meet the successor to Dr. Martin Luther King Jr. I am terribly excited.

I did get some mail today. I love walking down to the desk for our mail. Dina and I have each gotten mail everyday so far. I got a letter from Michael Bellesiles. I don't know him very well but it was a special letter. He included a quotation by Apache Chief Magnus Colorado, "Only people with empty heads feast while their hearts are heavy with grief."

I got a long letter from Nancy. I wanted her to be here. I know that she has to be home with her mother, but she deserves to see the women and the work here.

Nancy is one of the most important women in my life. She singled-handedly forced me to redefine feminism. She walked into the Magic Speller one day wearing high heels and perfume. I instantly dismissed her as I believed that feminists would never dress or look like that. Then she picked out many of my favorite and most radical books authored by Mary Daly, Shulamith Firestone and Andrea Dworkin. She talked and revealed that she is politically astute and committed. She cares deeply and acts on her commitments. She earned and won my trust, leaving me no choice but to abandon my tidy little categories.

I think she would love to see what is going on here. I wish my entire NOW chapter could see what is going on here. It would set their hearts on fire. After months of mailings, begging for donations, meetings and talks; they deserve to see this. They are the real power behind all of this. Thousands of women in little meetings all over the country, who want equality for their daughters, are the real source of our power. The energy in the Capitol is flowing from them and their belief in equality.

I just can't understand what is the big hold-up. Why aren't people utterly repulsed to be living under a constitution that does not explicitly state that all human beings are equal under the law? The current constitution is shameful. Why aren't people rushing to amend it, fix it, elevate it and move on to greater issues like full representation in government, equality in employment and education?

At this point, it doesn't even matter to me how this equality is applied. What matters is removing any and all obstacles to equality. Then, if a woman (or man) chooses a newly paved opportunity, it is her decision. Incredibly, Phyllis Schlafly is making progress against the amendment by suggesting that women will have to dig ditches as fast as men, women will have to carry adult men out of burning houses and, most heinous, use firearms in war.

This manipulation is unforgivable. Are we measuring masculinity by brute strength? That should infuriate men as much as women. I feel safe stating that every woman, pro or anti, wants her dentist and doctor to have a delicate touch, a gentle approach, a kind manner.

I know lots of women who can dig a ditch, but most are smart enough to enlist John Deere. I don't need every fireman (?) on the truck to be able to carry dad out of the burning barn – one will do. And has any one heard of Boudicca, the Celtic Queen who led an army against Claudius' Roman military? Diana, Nike, Joan, countless women who have been soldiers, pilots, samurai and many more whose patriotism required them to fight in full male disguise? They can cut off heads with the best of them. Besides it was often women who trained these little boys to wield their rage and it is women who make airplanes and war ordnance while the boys are busy killing.

But my real point is -- I don't care if women take on every role. What I DO care about is that the rules, be they height or weight or strength or agility or education or intelligence, do not exclude either gender. As long as gender is a lever for one sex to oppress and one sex to be oppressed, it must be fought.

Sunday, May 30
Day 13

As of today I have done three big E's. No one could have ever predicted I would do such a thing. It is so out of character for me that only the ERA, for all women for all time, could have made me do this. But the truly great news is that my vision has cleared entirely which means I am mobile again. Losing my independence had been just torture. I am very relieved.

This morning Dr. Alvenia Fulton arrived complete with a portable high colonic machine in hand. I have no idea how it works and I am not the least bit curious. Not one of us accepted her generous offer. Aside from her machine, she is infinitely interesting. She is tall and regal. She looks like an Egyptian priestess. Maybe it is the things she is talking about; ancient knowledge and nutrition information handed down. These topics have never been of much interest to me, but since I haven't eaten anything in thirteen days, I am somewhat receptive. But what have I missed? Did one of us expect her? Why is she here? How did she get here? Did Greg hire her to come here? It feels like some kind of secret society.

Dr. Fulton began with explaining that olive trees are the oldest known plants and that a person can live on olive oil alone; rubbed directly onto the skin. Natural grain and seeds hold the essence of life. Wheat was found in King Tut's tomb and although it had been buried over five thousand years ago, it is still alive. If you sprout grain and eat it, you are eating the very essence of life. She went on to explain that tumors live off of dead food and if you only eat live food you will never have tumors. She continued -- Do not eat cheese with cooked food such as pasta or bread. White potatoes, cheese and lettuce simply impact the colon. I have to admit that after not eating for thirteen days, my body is still eliminating fecal matter. I would have guessed it would be empty by now.

Right now our bodies are living off themselves. Stored toxins are coming out and with water constantly flushing out our system, we will enter an entirely new world in twenty-one days. Dr. Fulton said that any impurities, even cancer cells, cannot live past twenty-one days. She is saying bluntly that this will cure cancer. In addition, almond milk, made up of one cup ground almonds, three cups water and honey to taste, will prevent cancer.

Food seems very distant to me today. I have seen people eating: in restaurant windows, on the streets, in the rotunda. It seems like an option. Maybe a peculiar observation, but now it appears to be an expensive interruption. Three or four times a day life stops, money is spent and people eat. TV tells them what to eat and they eat. Is there any thinking involved at all? How much of it is a matter of choice? Blind, redundant thoughtless eating.

Monday, May 31
Day 14

Last night, after going to the movies and on to bed, Sonia was taken to the hospital. She was having a lot of trouble getting to the bathroom as her muscles were bothering her terribly. They ran some blood tests and concluded that it is a potassium deficiency, They gave her some pills for it and she came back to the Ramada Inn. Then again, this morning, she went back to the hospital with severe chest pains. They did an electrocardiogram which read normal. The doctor thinks it could have been a reaction to taking the pills.

Sonia said that she really liked her doctor. He is Canadian and will be "our doctor," if he can remain anonymous. It is a great boon to find a doctor who has no loyalty to the Illinois legislature. He is going to come by the motel and collect both urine and blood samples. He is very sympathetic to our position and will not charge anything except the lab fees for analysis.

Dina and I are not wavering about not getting involved with traditional medicine. I realize at this point our position is a luxury. However, I intend to be able to stick to it for as long as the fasts continues. I have called Adam several times. He is so helpful, knowledgeable, supportive. He has made calls to The East/West Institute and they have been totally reassuring. They have insisted that this is a healthy thing to be doing and to not be afraid of any of the residual symptoms. They will not last very long. In addition, I like talking with Adam. He is kind and a constant reminder that men can be gentle and supportive.

I had, at one point, decided that the lines of this battle had to be tightly drawn with men and women on separate sides. Then my life drew to me four astonishing men who would destroy the simplicity of my scheme. Adam is the most gentle man I have ever known. He isn't involved in the battle at all. Bruce is all heart and could never be an enemy. David had read more about the Women's Movement than almost any woman I know and has genuinely understood it. He is conversant on the works of Mary Daly and that is enough for me. Finally, there is Chuck. He is entirely open to the fact that women, as the oppressed class, are evolving; while men, as the oppressors, are not. I am astounded that these four men have stepped outside of the male group-consciousness. I can say they have permanently obscured my clear cut black and white lines. For me the big lesson here is that it only takes a few open hearts in a group to temper the heart of a staunch adversary.

Sonia came back in time to get ready to go to President Lincoln's tomb by 1:00 P.M. Dr. Joseph Lowry and a few other men arrived just before noon and off we went in the rain. We must be such a odd sight. Seven women, who are obviously strong political people, straggling in a thin and slow line. I think each of us has fallen into her own pace now. We are struggling to get from point A to point B and whether or not we arrive at the same time is no longer a concern. We can only concern ourselves with getting there. We are just frail women plodding along, accompanied by a group of strong and powerful men, hoping to say a few words about liberation.

It never occurred to me that the tomb would be in a cemetery. As silly as that sounds, the only president monuments I have ever seen are the Lincoln, Jefferson and

The Hungry Heart

Washington in the District of Columbia – none in a cemetery. Our line of vehicles wound around the Oak Ridge Cemetery passing hundreds of decorated graves. We parked next to a huge stone building with a tower. There are lots of bronze statues commemorating the Civil War, but the one that really stands out is an enormous head of Lincoln. His nose is bright and shiny as thousands of tourists rub it for good luck.

Walking around the back there is a iron gate on the vault entrance. Inside everything is marble and cold with more statues along a hallway. Finally we got to the sarcophagus chamber to discover wreaths on easels. Someone made arrangements to have chairs placed around the tomb. We each had one white rose to lay on the tomb. The press was there in full force including the local TV stations.

This picture is one I have dreamt of all my life. What happens when people, who are seeking liberation, come together? This is a moment I have been preparing for, wishing for, praying for, as long as I can remember. However I never ever would have imagined the stage and the players to be this grand, this articulate, this renown. Dr. Lowery knew Dr. Martin Luther King Jr. He knows Coretta Scott King. He said that he finds us inspiring. Does he know how inspired I am to meet him? Is that what is actually happening here? Does each seeker enkindle the flame of another? Does the Spirit of Liberation travel from one soul to another lighting a succession of souls?

So Mr. Lincoln, what have you done for us today and what must I do tomorrow?

Tuesday, June 1
Day 15

They keep asking me why am I here. They ask all of us why are we here. I want to know why they *aren't* here. Are they asking because they cannot believe someone cares enough to be doing this? I cannot believe they care so little. Today is a big turning point. Today we have fasted for two weeks. Today we have one month left to ratify the Equal Rights Amendment.

Eleven months ago the Countdown Campaign began with Ellie Smeal announcing that First Lady Betty Ford and Alan Alda would be the ERA Honorary Co-Chairs. There were 170 rallies in 42 states -- balloons, signs, cheers, mothers and daughters. I need them today. I need it all today. Over the last year thousands of us have staged marches, run phone banks, folded flyers, sealed envelopes, collected money and stood up to be counted. Many women quit their jobs and told their families they would be back in a year. Today I feel like there is only a handful of us pestering Springfield, Illinois.

I wonder if polling statistics have actually worked against us. Gallup says that 63 percent of Americans support the ERA. Presidents Ford and Carter have publicly spoken in favor of it. Are people complacent and staying home because they believe it cannot fail? Not that I make a habit of reading

The Hungry Heart

Glamour magazine, but in May 1981 they reported that thirty-three percent of the people who responded picked the ERA as their top concern. Second was a woman's right to a safe and legal abortion. As much as I am glad that so many feel this way, I worry that these kinds of numbers lull people into believing that the ERA is a done deal.

I have also read opinion pieces in the paper that we may lose because we believe the ERA is right, moral and just. Well pardon me. Is this an indictment that we are naïve? Later this summer I will be thirty-four and, naïve or not, I am not willing to abandon three central ideas; 1) people are equal, 2) Americans create their government and 3) I am responsible. I did not just make this up. I did not just invent the idea of equality. It is the minimal expression of morality and justice. For me the obvious question is, if government is not just and moral, then aren't I obligated to change the government? I can't accept that morality and my government are mutually exclusive. It is simply a greater call to conscience.

I imagine that some people think this is about being lesbian. That's just because they don't know any better. I don't think that one gender is fundamentally morally superior. I do see that men are holding the line on guaranteeing their own rights and excluding women. Does this mean that women will have to integrate government and justice? It looks that way, now doesn't it?

I have done a great deal of thinking about this – reading about this – writing about this. In graduate school it just seemed to come into focus. Possibly it was the natural product of combining the broken promises of Vatican II, Gandhi's *My Experiments with Truth*, Gustavo Gutierrez's *Liberation Theology* and radical feminism. In particular, Mary Daly's phrase, "God is a Verb," broke open my mind and heart. (She is and will always be a linchpin in my life. I love her.)

I believe that advancement, as illustrated by a giraffe stretching to reach the best leaves, always seeks light, something better, something freer. It is the act of stretching that is the imitation of god. Another way of saying this is that god is within us, joins with us and moves us to freedom, liberation, justice. To my mind, this is the actual prayer a human offers – a conscious life longing and working for light.

Those who are pushing down, those who are pushing back, those who are confining and limiting are diminishing morality, justice and light. It isn't that one gender is morally superior, it is that now in my lifetime, it is the men who are oppressing and the women who are oppressed. And more importantly my awareness obligates me to do all I can to break this cycle.

I cannot wait for anyone else to agree. I cannot wait for others to join me. I cannot pout if left alone. My heart drives my life.

Maybe women are complacent because it was men who voted in the Nineteenth Amendment and appear to be including women. In reality, women have not stepped up to their voting power. Men and women may vote in presidential elections in equal numbers, but it is not representative of the population. And even among the women who do vote, they are not wielding any political leverage. They do not demand fair labor laws, secure child protection or even elect women in representative numbers. In fact, political savvy is often labeled as masculine behavior, unattractive and anti-family. Surely Representative Bella wears those natty hats, not just with great panache, but with deep wisdom.

Any accusation that women are not smart or political enough to stand toe-to-toe with men, equally under the law, is not only inaccurate but immoral. A wide-eyed survey of any U.S. neighborhood reveals more women in the workplace. More women in politics. More women teaching. More women heads of households. None of this is by reward. This is by necessity. Women are needed to work, govern, teach and lead their families into the future. Clearly they need constitutional equality.

Today Ellie Smeal issued a statement that the insurance industry is the primary opponent. They stand to lose the most if gender discrimination becomes illegal, so they are spending millions to defeat the amendment. They want to continue charging women higher rates and granting unequal benefits. NOW says that women pay more for health and disability insurance even though women have shorter hospital stays and fewer injuries on the job.

Is the government actually going to exclude women from the Constitution? How could that be? I think Speaker Ryan needs to phone Supreme Court Justice Sandra Day O'Connor to apologize for not including her in the Constitution.

Wednesday, June 2
Day 16

Three different legislators are threatening to vote no on the rules change if we don't stop the fast. Senator Forest Etheridge came to the Ramada Inn last night and pulled a predictable trick out of the OLD BOY's bag. The meeting was to be completely off the record and we were to tell no one. We convened in the motel conference room. He was late and we waited. I was furious. I don't care who he is and that he is an elected official; it was ugly and manipulative.

He acted as if he was on a mission directly from God. He said that as a Catholic, he was ultimately concerned about our health. He pouted and whined as if true care had brought him to that moment. So now, out of love and concern for us, he is going to vote no on the three-fifths rules change if we don't stop the fast. Senator James Taylor, the sponsor of the ERA, has postponed the vote because of this odious move.

What on earth did he really expect from coming over here? Did he think we would just walk out of the meeting and announce that we have thought it over and decided that fasting is foolish? Did he think that we would bow to his infinite wisdom, see the light and call it off? And who exactly sent him? I wish the others had not been so solicitous and respectful with him. He folded his hands and, with a heavy heart, asked us what our intentions are. He seemed to believe that we had sinister and secret motives and that we would be relieved to confide in him -- like baring our conscience. Did he think we believed that this meeting was private and confidential? How ridiculous. AND insulting!

Nonetheless, one by one, we told him who we are and where we are from. He sat at the head of the table as if he were Clifton Webb, in *Cheaper by the Dozen*, waiting to carve the turkey. I disliked that scene at home and I am not enchanted by it today. What a smug, arrogant, calculating man. The final fallout of this little drama is that now he can say that a) he did his best, b) no need to change the three-fifths rule because c) the fasters are blocking the amendment.

Later that day, after everyone slept a little bit and got a handle on what actually happened, we wrote a statement telling the entire country what is happening here. We all marched into the pressroom and issued a statement.

For Immediate Release:

We are here to make eminently clear again the purpose and intent of this spiritual fast. Because of the multitude of questions being asked by the press, we decided the most expedient way to respond would be with this press conference.

The events of the past week prove more conclusively than anything we can possibly say that we are indeed accomplishing what we set out to do two and a half weeks ago: to present a spiritual witness to women's hunger for justice. First in the chain of events, Speaker Ryan adjourned the House for an unprecedented 10 days at the end of the session, and second, Senators and Representatives are being pressured at this moment to change their "yes" votes to "no" in an all out effort to stop this fast. If the fast were not effective, would such an action be necessary? Why else would it seem necessary to deliberately misrepresent the purpose and meaning of the fast as has been done so frequently?

Many of you have asked us what we intend to do about these lawmakers who so easily abandon their principle and so easily lay pressure. It is not for us to monitor their consciences. We intend to do what we came here to do: to witness the truth of the principle of equality for all Americans.

Indeed, if legislators have genuine concern for our health, the obvious and quickest route to preserving it is for them to vote immediately for the majority rule and for the ratification of the ERA. Any other response seems to us hypocritical, patronizing, and ultimately insincere.

We are here representing millions of women who hunger for justice. Let us suppose legislators truly disagree with the fasting of seven women in Springfield, does that justify their compromising democratic principles, by turning their backs on the desperate hunger of all American women seeking justice? Such lack of principled action only deepens our conviction that we are desperately needed here to continue our solemn spiritual witness to this legislature and to the Governor.

When Lois Becker Frolova fasted recently in order to have her husband released from the Soviet Union, she was applauded by Vice President George Bush and heralded as a woman with "intestinal fortitude." Why, when women fast for the rights of men, is it considered more acceptable and sacred than when women fast for the rights of women? Why is ours called "political extortion" and hers considered an "act of heroism?" It is of course, because women's rights are not taken seriously. That is why we are here: to testify to the seriousness and sacredness of the women's cause.

After the press conference, we went to our usual place in the rotunda. It was jammed. The stop ERA ladies, dressed in red & white, were out droves. I just cannot believe that their issue is economics. They look like they shop at Marshall Fields and have grown children. They do not look like they are the principle wage earner in their homes. Could it be that they don't know anyone who needs this amendment? I would like to give them the benefit of the doubt, but how could they not know anyone who would benefit from the ERA? Are none of their daughters in law school or applying to law school? And have they figured out what they will do when they are widowed and their social security is only a portion of what their husbands paid in?

I am willing to listen and see what they are fighting for, but the fact is I really don't understand it. Their primary objections are unfounded and unintelligent. They say they want men and women to remain different. There is no legislation that could remove the essential, inherent differences of men and women.

The ERA is not going to require the integration of American toilets. It won't make it illegal for men and women to pee separately in restaurants. Airplanes and most homes will continue to offer unisex toilets.

So I just sat in my folding chair, last seat on the left and who should appear but the Queen of them all, Phyllis Schlafly. All the way from Alton, Illinois, all the way from the last century, all the way from the far right; there she was wearing a pink silk dress, single strand of pearls and Stop ERA stickers on her back. I have to admit the women on her side are looking a lot better than we are these days.

The press was going crazy. Without a second thought, I grabbed my little camera and walked over to her. It was so funny. Everyone stepped aside as I stood just two feet in front of her. I had gotten one of the guards to buy an Illinois postcard for me and asked Phyllis to sign it. You would have thought I had asked her to sign the ERA right then and there. Her aides whispered in her ear and she in theirs. She asked me what I was going to do with the card. I told her that I would put it in my scrapbook and that I considered her to be a women of genuine historical significance. She was very cordial. She signed it. I thanked her. I went back to my seat.

Some press people came over to me and told me that if I had given them a moment's notice, they would have photographed our exchange. Gee, that wasn't what I wanted. I just wanted to meet her and ask for her autograph. I didn't want a scene. No matter the issue or what side either of us hold, she is a woman of great power and has designed her own liberation. She is passionate and dedicated. I admire her commitment.

When everyone got home I was able to drive Dixie's car by myself. I do love being alone. I went to the post office and had a great time in a dusty bookstore. I bought a used edition of Dickinson's poetry. It is illustrated and signed by Nancy Ekholm Burkert. It was $25.00.

Tonight we all went to see the movie, *Victor/Victoria*. Everyone loved it. The NOW guards went with us. The lobby was a little scary: popcorn, Junior Mints, Milk Duds, Jujyfruits, Sno-caps, Chuckles, Goobers, Good'N Plenty and Raisinettes!

Tonight, as I was writing in my red and white polka dot blank book, the phone rang. It was Gloria Steinem. The switchboard had accidentally transferred Sonia's call to our room. She called to say that she would like to pay for the rental of a fifteen passenger van so we can get around as a unit; wheelchairs and all.

Thursday, June 3
Day 17

DAY OF REBELLION

If there is a day in this half of the century that women can be proud of, today is the day. I want to call everyone I know and tell them, "Today is the Day!" Today women disobeyed the law for my rights. These are brave women. These are women of change. These are the best of my gender. I love them furiously.

We knew in advance about their plans and did not go to the rotunda today. We conferred and all agreed, fasters and chainers alike, that it would be best to not risk being arrested. We knew that if the police made a wide sweep through the Capitol they would not differentiate between the chainers and the fasters. Most likely, they would just arrest all of us. No one wants us to be fasting in jail. The ACLU is poised to move on our behalf to block forced feeding, but it would be better to not be in custody. Even so, I wish I could have seen it.

This morning seventeen women walked directly up to the third floor of the Capitol and chained themselves to the railing around the entrance of the Illinois State Senate.

Their statement:

> These chains we use symbolize the legal, economic and social chains that still bind women today. We seek to disrupt the sluggish and unresponsive process that has dragged on for so many years and demand that the legislature act immediately to ratify the ERA.

They said they would stay chained until they decide it is time to leave. While these brave women were chanting in the Capitol, hundreds were outside the building at a rally. Charlotte Bunch and Wilma Scott Heide spoke to the crowd.

It is 9:30 P. M. and we heard they are still on the third floor chained to the Senate doors. The police have made an interesting move by ignoring them. The building officials have told the press that the women can stay as long as they like. They will not be forcibly removed.

One at a time, the women unchain themselves to use the rest room. Right now it seems that it will be a matter of how long they can last. Since they are prepared and have been practicing for weeks, I think they could stay there indefinitely.

Senator Etheredge appeared on the TV news tonight and said, "Where does it end? Are we going to have people threaten to slash their wrists unless the legislature passes a certain appropriation bill?" Is he kidding? Could he really be comparing the Equal Rights Amendment to the Constitution of the United States to an appropriation bill? Is he representing the sentiment of the Illinois Senate? And does he see these women as extortionists or people making suicide threats?

The organizers of the group are Mary Lee Sargent and Kari Alice Lynn. They have been getting ready for months. They practiced chaining and unchaining themselves so no one could prevent them from completing their action once they got to the third floor.

Their flyer:

THE PURPOSE OF THE DAY

1. To let the legislation know that we will hold each and every member accountable for its shameful failure to ratify the ERA.
2. To convince legislators to reconsider their position on the ERA and the 3/5ths rule.
3. To express the bonds of sisterhood and solidarity with all who work for equality and the ERA.
4. To demonstrate that legislators' actions have only strengthened our resolve to keep fighting.
5. To express our anger.
6. To cause embarrassment and frustration to our oppressors.

The History of the Day:

Winning the vote for American women entailed a 72-year struggle* and success came only after suffragists began engaging in direct, confrontative tactics. Women's suffrage was a moribund issue when the final push was begun in 1910 by women who had witnessed the militant tactics of Emmeline Pankhurst and her daughters, Cristibel and Sylvia, in their efforts to gain suffrage in Great Britain.

Alice Paul was among these women. The day before Woodrow Wilson's 1912 inauguration, Paul organized a demonstration in Washington D.C. Her strategy: to hold the party in power accountable. Moderate suffragists were skeptical. Undeterred, Paul formed the Women' s Party.

When America entered World War I, Women's Party members began picketing the White House. After a few months, the Wilson Administration, embarrassed by the women's actions, moved against them. Ninety-seven women were illegally arrested for "obstructing sidewalk traffic."

In prison, Alice Paul, Lucy Burns, Dorothy Day and others again borrowed British tactics. They demanded to be treated like political prisoners and went on a hunger strike. Paul's lasted for 22 days and a doctor who examined her reported, "This is a spirit like Joan of Arc and it is useless to try and change it. She will die but she will never give up."

Released from prison, the suffragists resumed their picketing. Women's Party tactics paid off. The suffrage amendment was at last forced out of the House Rules Committee where it had been bottled up for years. On August 26, 1920, American women gained the right to vote. The Women's Party then dedicated itself to seeking an Equal Rights Amendment to the U.S. Constitution.

It has now been 59 years since that amendment was first introduced into Congress. Many of us are convinced it is long past time to follow in the courageous footsteps of our foremothers in the present struggle. "They" will never give us anything. It is up to us to claim it. In the words of Emmeline Pankhurst, "Remember the dignity of your womanhood. Do not appeal, do not beg, do not grovel. Take courage, join hands, stand beside us, fight with us."

Here I sit in luxury -- a motel room, TV, warm bed, convenient bathroom, pillows and jammies. They are sitting on a cold marble floor with no sleeping bags or blankets. Both of our groups want the same thing. All we are asking for is equality of rights under the law.

The original flyer included a typo of a 5-year struggle which is corrected here to state 72-year struggle (1848 – 1920) to win the vote.

Friday, June 4
Day 18

I heard President Reagan say that he is for the E and for the R, but not for the A. Is that a cheer from some junior high school? When the public hears that, do they nod their heads as if they understand? Is it so digestible because it is short and catchy? Men (and some women) have been standing in front of microphones, smiling and delivering this alphabetical answer with assurance and pride. I need them to spend one afternoon in Sister Caroline's eighth grade civics class. She would be able to explain indisputably the role of the United States Constitution and its purview.

In addition, Sister Caroline would firmly state, with ruler in hand, that we live in a democracy. When the majority of adults support an amendment, their elected legislative representatives are supposed to support it too. This would be particularly true when the issue is the identification and protection of human rights. As Sister proudly taught, the U.S. Constitution is the standard for human rights, the moral and elevated gauge for all the world to see and admire. When the truth is universal and elementary, it is worthy of becoming the law of the land. It warrants inclusion in the U.S. Constitution, thus establishing and guaranteeing human rights in all fifty states.

Then Sister Angelica, the math teacher, could offer a few words. If women make 59¢ compared to men making a dollar, shouldn't the same car cost 41% less for women? It is equally important for a mother or a father to have a safe car. If someone drives a $10,000 car to work, why is it a fifth of his $50,000 annual income and a third of her comparable pay? Or is she supposed to buy a $6,000 car -- a fifth of her $30,000? Work is work. Equal pay for equal work. This is something that any seven year old set of boy-girl twins can explain at allowance time. There is no way you can give Jack a dollar and Jill 59¢.

I am certain that Sister Jean Marie, the religion teacher, would have some trouble with the language of the amendment. I am actually a bit conflicted about it myself. I have wished that the amendment be changed to use the word, "gender" instead of "sex." If the twenty three words were, *Equality of rights under the law shall not be denied or abridged by the United States or any state on account of gender*, I feel confident that the jittery embarrassed arguments about homosexuality, marriage and abortion would disappear. I believe that some people are simply emotional about the word sex. They can't calmly discuss it with their family or neighbors.

The ironic thing is that most of my education has been by these sisters. These are educated women who belong to matriarchal communities. Their founders and leaders have been articulate, powerful, published, inspired, deeply intelligent women. Their communities establish, direct and maintain thousands of hospitals, schools and charities. They may be under the rule of the Pope and dedicate their lives to a church that bestows second class citizenship on them, but their example shone through. Women are leaders. Women are capable. Women are worth educating. Women can develop and run institutions effectively.

Looking beyond the alcoholism, the loneliness, the empty life of my mother, I always saw her intelligence. In her case it was wasted intelligence. She graduated from college in 1931 and never worked. She would not let me get a summer job while in high school because , as she told me, girls did not work. I escaped boredom and circled around her admonition by doing volunteer work forty hours a week at a hospital for three summers. While her widowhood came early and her estate sustained her scotch and solitude for thirty years, I knew she was smarter than most men and would have found fulfillment in a professional career. She was trapped by her belief that it was not suitable for a woman to be in business. I believe she was as much a victim of the patriarchal legislature as any woman. She was my teacher too.

Saturday, June 5
Day 19

It is Saturday and The Grassroots Group of Second Class Citizens is still on the third floor of the State Capitol. Someone brought them sleeping bags Friday morning. The Senate did not meet Friday and the officials are saying that they can stay indefinitely. Friday was a particularly dark day; North Carolina permanently tabled the ERA in a 27-23 vote. That state is lost.

The loss refueled the women here. Fourteen of the original seventeen are still in their chains and are determined more than ever to stay. We, fasters, did the impossible this morning -- we went to a grocery store. Up until that moment, we were living in a state of denial; to our thinking, there simply was no food on the planet. But today we went to an IGA and bought food for the fourteen women who are chained to the Senate doors. And there is a lot of food on the planet.

When we got there, it was quite a scene. With Mary and Sonia in wheelchairs, we all piled into the elevator and hit the "3." The doors opened and we were galvanized, mesmerized, dazzled, blinded. We looked at them and they looked at us. It was the most poetic moment I have ever felt in the women's movement. I should say, a moment worthy of poetry. I am inspired by us. I am inspired by them. I am humbled and privileged to be a person capable of inspiring their spirits. Then we stepped out of the elevator, shattering the frozen holy moment. We laughed and talked and mostly just looked at each other. There was so much unspoken. We stood in history carrying on the work of Pankhurst, Sanger, Paul, Stanton and Anthony. For the few hours that we were together there was no way to be glib or pretend that we didn't realize just who we were and who had come before us. It feels as if the petty human being goes away and something much larger and more powerful stands proud and shines through. I am awestruck by what has been surging in and through me.

No matter how life goes, or what tasks I must do to survive in the Twentieth Century, evolution swells forward. I am her daughter and her device through which she evolves.

My friend and photographer, Judy Rosenfeld arrived at 2 P.M. We have agreed to call her J. R. to differentiate between her and Judy Block. I took Dixie's car and picked her up. Georgia, Helen and Helen's sons flew here with her. They have come in time for the big rally tomorrow. The motel they are staying in is not very nice, but Helen's boys will love the video games. We dropped them off and J.R. and I went on to the Ramada. I am so happy J.R. is here, I love her. I feel safe with her.

She is right next door, sharing a room with Mary. Although she is self-conscious about smoking, I love the smell of her cigarettes. After she ate dinner she was further embarrassed that Dina and I could tell her exactly what she ate. We can smell everything, right down to the mustard. J.R. brought all of her equipment, even a portable dark room. Because of her bad back and neck trouble, she wears a big camera strap around her middle instead of one that hangs around her neck.

Mary's room is rather grim. She hasn't opened the windows or curtains since we arrived. Her kidneys are really bothering her and she is very concerned about the possible long term physical damage. She has three small children and wants to avoid any unnecessary risks. Today she decided she wanted some expert advice from Dr. Paul Bragg, the author of many books on fasting. She call the Bragg Institute in Hawaii and asked to speak to Paul. It seems he has been dead for several years! We laughed like crazy birds! I think J.R. will help her a lot. J.R. can make anyone laugh.

Tonight we performed a Full Moon Ritual that I have been working on for the last week. I put this ceremony together to offer some balance to the Catholic services that Maureen has brought us. She has done wonderful work and we all appreciate the letter of support she solicited from twenty-three American Bishops. My thinking is that we should have all types of prayer and worship represented. Our history is much older than the Judeo-Christian tradition. I want to acknowledge the time before patriarchy took over religion.

I have never done this type of thing before, but it needs to be done. I feel a bit odd about it because I don't want to be labeled in any religion: pagan, witchcraft or Christianity. I just want it all. Actually I don't want any attention on my beliefs. I think they are too non-traditional and would ultimately isolate me.

I called Starhawk in San Francisco for inspiration and direction. She gave me some chants to use. The moon is full tonight in early Sagittarius. When it got dark we gathered in the field behind the motel and formed a circle around a bowl of water and salt.

The Hungry Heart

RITUAL OF POWER AND FREEDOM

The circle is cast; the ritual has begun. We have created sacred space. A space fit for the Goddess to enter. We have cleansed ourselves and centered ourselves; out mental bonds have dropped away. Free from fear, we can open to the moon and starlight. In perfect love and trust, we are prepared to evoke the Goddess.

GROUP BREATHING	Breathe deeply and turn the air into light and power. Exhale slowly. (5 times)
GROUNDING	To become grounded and guard against being drained, we are going to become radiant pillars of solid energy stretched between Mother Earth and the planets. • Place you feet firmly on the earth • Straighten your back • Feel the energy flow up and down • Draw in the earth's vitality
CONE OF POWER	This base is the circle of women. The apex is the moon. Hold hands and raise them while visualizing a clockwise circle of light. Hold the image as it glows brighter and brighter.
CHANT	We are the flow. We are the ebb. We are the weavers. We are the web. (5 times)

• Going around the circle counter clockwise, Tell us when you first felt powerless.
• Watch the words flow into the bowl of saltwater, the ocean, the feminine, as it is transformed.
• After all have spoken, pass the bowl around, take a drink.
• Pour the rest into the earth.

CHANT   We can rise with the fire of freedom.
         Truth is the fire that burns our chains.
         We can stop the fire of oppression.
         Healing is the fire running though our veins.
         (3 times)

INVOCATION   Let us ask the sun to warm us.
              Let us ask the rain and cold to support us by
              waiting until we are done.

CHANT   We are all one with the infinite sun, forever, and
         ever and ever.
         We are in tune with the luminous moon, forever
         and ever and ever.
         (5 times)

GROUND   Pour the excess power into the earth. Giving
          back whatever you do not need.

BUILD A   Visualize the circle as a solid and protected ring
PERMANENT   which nothing negative can pierce.
PSYCHIC
WALL

CHANT   She changes everything she touches and
         Everything she touches changes.
         We are changers.
         Everything we touch can change.
         (5 times)

I am not sure if they think I am crazy but at the very least, we were not asking a male god to make everything better for us. I believe that we were asking our best selves to step forward and take personal responsibility. Now if power does come forward, when power does come forward, we have an option of believing that it came from the Woman Spirit that lives within us.

Sunday, June 6
Day 20

I woke up exhausted and had to collect myself. Today there are major ERA rallies in the four state Capitals that are waiting for a vote: Tallahassee, Florida; Raleigh, North Carolina; Oklahoma City, Oklahoma and Springfield, Illinois. This is everyone's last chance to express their feelings of support for the ERA in an organized way.

Our first activity was a prayer service at Iles Park at 9:00 A.M. We were in the van and on the way by 8:45. It was surprising to find the park already filled with supporters. We had expected crowds to show up for the march at 11:00 A.M., but not for the prayer service. The ritual itself was another beseeching a male god to fix things.

After the service, we crammed into the van. We waited a long time for a break in traffic. While I was staring blankly out the window, I saw Rebecca! She came all the way from St. Louis for the march and to see me. The windows on the van didn't open and my wild waving didn't get her attention. We pulled away and all I could do was hope to find her at the rally. I think it has been seven years since I have seen her. She has two daughters now and I have not met either of them.

We went back to the motel for awhile. There was no reason for us to wait around for the march -- none of us could make the two hour walk to the Capitol. We heard that it is a good thing we did leave, as a man had been arrested earlier in the park, carrying seven knives with each of our names carved on them. I sure am glad they found him before he found any of us. What a creepy thing to know and feel. For the rest of my life I will know that a man had a knife with "Zoe" carved on it. I know he really doesn't want to kill me at all. He wants to kill all women who want liberation. He wants to kill equality.

Our van took off for the Capitol at 12:30 P.M. Eight fasters, three aides and four NOW bodyguards. For some reason we were feeling particularly weak and sensitive today and the helpers had their hands full. We drove to the rear entrance and went in to the Capitol from the basement. The Secret Service was on duty because First Lady Betty Ford was there.

Walking into the rotunda, we all felt very strange. It was entirely empty with an echo and, yet, we knew that the chainers were just two stories above us and we really wanted to see them. All of the various security people: secret service, police and state officials have forbidden us to go anywhere in the Capitol but outside the door to the rally.

We straggled into the rotunda on foot and in wheelchairs and began to sing to the women two floors above us, "We'll never give up. We'll never give in." They hung their heads over the railing and sang with us to the tune of the National Anthem, *"Equality of rights under the law shall not be denied or abridged by the United States or by any state on account of sex."*

It was a quiet moment. It was a fantastic moment. It was heart. It was my heart joining with every other woman's heart. Even women who are afraid of being equal, even women who are afraid of self-reliance, all women. Women in overalls. Women in aprons. Women in the Olympics. Women in the fields. Our singing swirled around this round proud ceiling and filled the heart of the Mother Goddess Spirit.

The Hungry Heart

We walked the fifty feet to the east Capitol steps and looked out the door; a gigantic wave of light and energy crashed and poured over us. Five thousand women in a sea of green and white stood in front of us, cheering us, clapping for us. They were singing and chanting and deserving equality of rights under the law.

A special space had been set for us. The rally was three hours long. There were speeches and songs. Ellie Smeal, Mayor Jane Byrne and Betty Ford spoke. From where I sat, I could not hear what they said.

In the crowd I saw Ruby. I wanted to call to her, hug her, but the security was stern and thick and would not let me venture into the crowd. I had forgotten just how inventive Ruby is and within ten minutes, she was standing right next to me on the stage. Such a great joyous thing to see an old friend. Then, somehow, Rebecca got through and sat with me for a long time. Art wasn't with her but he intends to visit next Sunday. They are going to bring the girls.

The speeches continued on and on and soon it came time for us to speak. Addressing five thousand people was like nothing I ever imagined. We had one minute each. "Before I left California I asked a friend, who had stopped smoking eight years ago, when will the desire go away? She said that when it happens, she will let me know. And so it is with our hunger for justice. It will never go away until we win equality for all."

1. Maria was the most beautiful woman I have ever seen. And she loved me! Surprised in love.

2. Irene (Maria's Mom) & Maria, Mom & me. A very unlikely quartet.

3. Maria and I lived over the Magic Speller Bookstore in Newport Beach, CA and were the envy of every bibliophile.

4. We bought a button machine and made hundreds. These say -- 365 Days until the ERA.

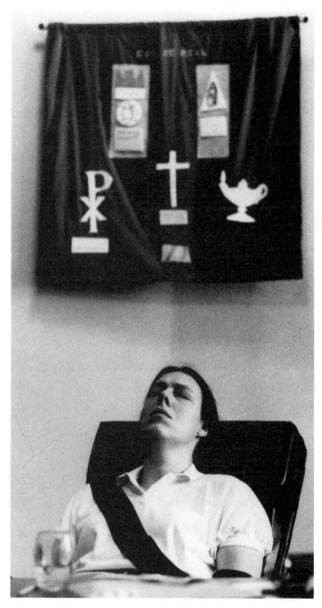

5. Sitting in the workroom at Kumler Methodist Church, all I want to do is close my eyes. I have a terrible unrelenting headache until I start drinking a lot more water. *May 21*

6. The Day of Rebellion. Women chain themselves to the Senate Chamber doors.
Five women in the center, (L to R) Sue Yarber, Kari Alice Lynn, Mary Lee Sargent,
Joyce Meyers, & Alice Webber. *June 3*

7. Fasters visit Chainers. In chairs, Sonia Johnson & Mary Barnes.
Seated on floor, (L to R) Charlotte Bunch, Kari Alice Lynn & Joyce Meyers.

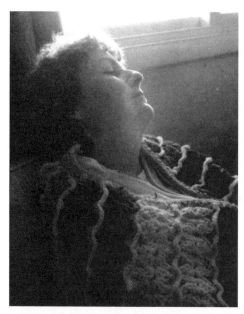

8. Mary Barnes could not get warm. Her room was always dark and her kidneys bothered her terribly. *June 5*

9. Sitting in the van at Iles Park, I spot friends who have come for the day. *June 6*

10. ERA rally at the Capitol. Betty Ford & Ellie Smeal are speakers.
Maureen is at the podium and we each get to say a line or two. *June 6*

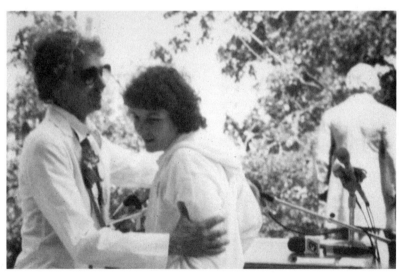

11. Dixie helps Mary back to her wheelchair after she speaks at the rally. *June 6*

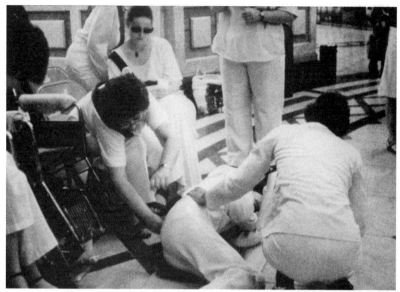

12. After not eating for 21 days, Sonia falls to the rotunda floor.
She is taken by ambulance to the hospital. *June 7*

13. Mary Lee and Kari Alice stand proud and strong in the rotunda.
One of the few times they are not in actual chains.

14. This young woman stood and stared at us for a very long time. We just couldn't believe how disgusted some women were with us.
June 10

15. In addition to trusting God, this demonstrator has added a little sign on top - Eat for the ERA.
June 10

16. A Stop ERA man is instructing his students about us.
June 10

17. Stop ERA and ERA YES stand shoulder to shoulder in the trenches.
June 10

18. ERA CAN GO AWAY HUNGRY
Just one of the many signs we faced everyday. *June 10*

19. I love ice cream. It looks better everyday. *June 10*

20. A huge rally in the rotunda celebrating Women and the ERA. *June 16*

21. Kristen Lems performs at the ERA rally. *June 16*

22. Dina (left) and I look out at our brave NOW guard. *June 16*

23. Dixie Johnson is our compass,
our protector, our pilot.

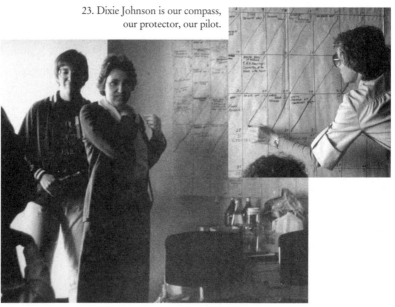

24. Kathy and Ellie arrive at Dixie's room for a strategy meeting. *June 17*

25. Alice Cohan and Ellie Smeal meet with us in Dixie's room at the Ramada Inn. *June 17*

26. Ellie Smeal, Dixie Johnson, Sue Yarber and Mary Lee Sargent strategize with us. *June 17*

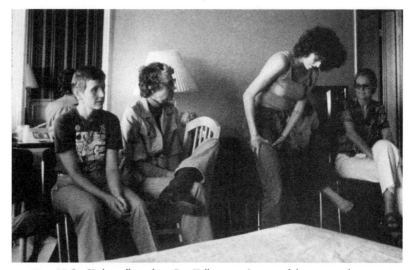

27. Sue Yarber tells us about Rep Kelley stomping two of the women who stormed the House on June 15. *June 17*

28. Shirley visits with her two sons; one anti-ERA and one pro-ERA. *June 18*

29. GGSCC is sitting in front of Speaker Ryan's doors. Dixie and I are peeking out of the nurses office down the hall. *June 18*

30. I asked J. R. to take this picture for Maria. MAD was Maria's favorite comic relief. *June 21*

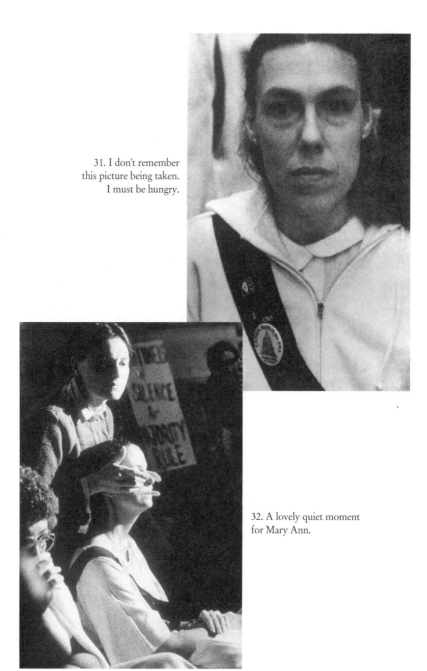

31. I don't remember
this picture being taken.
I must be hungry.

32. A lovely quiet moment
for Mary Ann.

33. This beautiful statue is dedicated to the Women of Illinois.
They need more than dusting -- they need the ERA.

34. Dina and I read names on a long petition for the Equal Rights Amendment.

35. For a fleeting moment, we hope as Florida House votes YES 60-58. *June 21*

36. The ERA is lost. Judy comforts Dina at a meeting in Dixie's room. *June 21*

37. Florida has voted and we sit on the lawn and grieve.
Dina and Sonia pour out their hearts. *June 21*

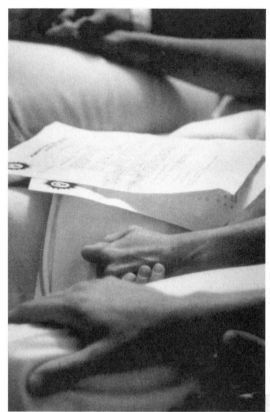

38. Prayer meeting at
First Presbyterian Church.
Held hands afraid to let go.
June 22

39. We raise
our hearts and hands
in prayer at First
Presbyterian Church
June 22

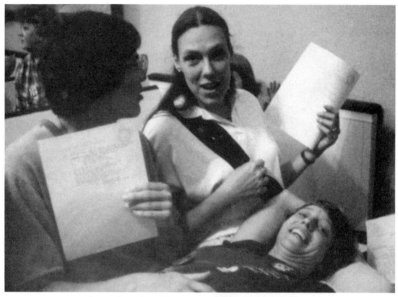

40. Kathy, Vicki and I celebrate our sisterhood at the Prayer meeting
at First Presbyterian Church *June 22*

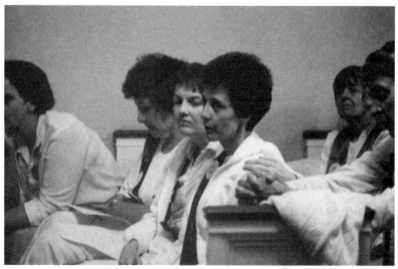

41. Sonia, Mary & Shirley attend the Prayer meeting at First Presbyterian Church *June 22*

42. The moment we have dreamt of - The IGA. *June 22*

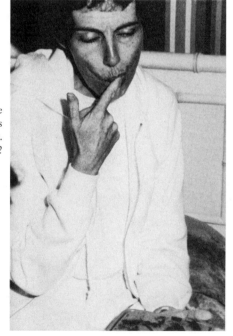

43. Sonia is in reverie over Dr. Fulton's fruit compote. *June 22*

44. Dixie, Kathy and I are having fun at the NOW campaign office on our last night in Illinois. *June 23*

45. Dina and I toast one another. The fast is over. *June 24*

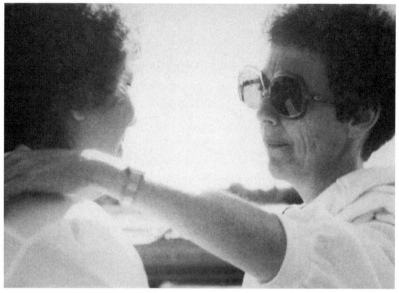

46. Sonia says goodbye to Mary at the Ramada Inn. *June 24*

47. All hugs. There is nothing more to do but say goodbye. *June 24*

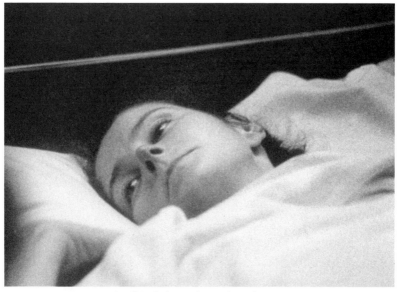

48. Mary Ann is still in the hospital, as we begin leaving town. *June 24*

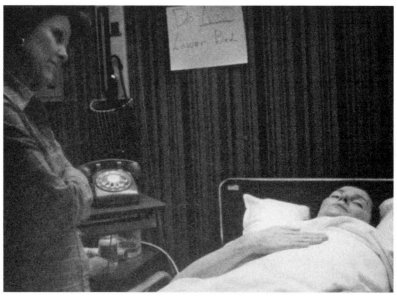

49. Dina says goodbye to Mary Ann. *June 24*

50. They surprise us at the airport! I love them with all my heart. *June 24*

CREDITS

Monday, June 7
Day 21

A day can pass and feel as if nothing happened and then one comes along that holds a lifetime within. Today was such a day.

At 3:45 A.M. the state guards, armed with guns and bolt cutters crashed onto the third floor of the Capitol. They unchained the women, picked them up, carried them outside, opened the dumpster and dropped them in with all of their belongings. Fifteen women were removed by force in the dark of early morning. No press, no warning, no discussion. This is actually fantastic news. This validates what Gandhi told us, the oppressors will indict themselves. The satyagrahis never have to concern themselves with demonstrating that the oppressors are without conscience. The exposure will unfold naturally in the process itself.

We arrived at the Capitol at the usual time, 11:00 A.M. and, without a word, went and sat in our familiar order. Helen and Georgia got there shortly after. They spotted us and simply stood there. Some fifty feet away, they just stood there. Their faces revealed a reverence that I have for the fasters in my own heart. It was quite a sight. I may be sitting here, last seat on the left, but I too can stand back and revere what is happening. Three wheelchairs today. Our honor guard, directed by NOW, has grown to a dozen or more women dressed in green and white who just want to stand with us. The press coverage is increasing too. *Life* magazine has sent Annie Lebowitz. The press is allowed inside of the circle to kneel or squat and ask questions. Around noon a film crew came in. It is a group of women who have been traveling across the U.S. documenting the ERA campaign. They asked each of us questions. They hope to sell their film to public television. Wouldn't it be wonderful if we had film of Stanton, Paul and Anthony?

Sonia did not have much to say today. She is very weak and she began complaining of nausea this morning. All of a sudden, Sonia slid off her chair and fell to the floor. She just ran out of energy and couldn't sit up any longer. Someone called an ambulance. It was just terrifying. The rest of us sat in silence. It wasn't that Sonia was in serious trouble or even that it would threaten the fast, but it was the beginning of our increasing, debilitating vulnerability. Our fight would have to be fought by others. Up until now, we had been acting and appearing as one and now part of us is no longer able to hold up her piece of the firmament. One of us has run out of strength. One of us is lying on the floor. We are all lying on the floor.

Shirley and Dixie went to the hospital with Sonia. While waiting in the emergency room, Shirley fainted. I am sure that her devotion to Sonia added to her already shaky condition. They are not back yet, but we hear that they are all going to be okay.

In the meantime, the GGSCC (Grassroots Group of Second Class Citizens) had gone into the Senate while they were in session. They lined the gallery and began chanting, "Our business before you business." They unfurled an American flag, draping it over the railing, invoking a great tradition of

Alice Paul, et al. The speaker gave them five minutes to stop. When they did not stop, the Senate adjourned.

The original plan had been for all of the fasters to sit in the House gallery today, but only five of us were able. NOW women had been sitting in seats since opening to reserve them for us. We sat on the Republican side to show our support for the sponsor of the amendment, Susan Catania.

Today was the "Committee of the Whole." This is a special arrangement to discuss an issue in front of the entire electoral body instead of small subcommittees. First seven women testified in favor of the amendment: Ellie Smeal, Dina, two attorneys and a woman from the Pentagon who addressed the draft. The facts are that Congress decides who is subject to the draft. It has always been that way. They can change the age limits or the gender lines within their own voting process. The U.S. Constitution has no authority on the draft and the ERA does not affect it.

Then it was time for the opponents to speak. All heads turned to the door and in walked a line of dotted-swiss, crinolined, virginal little darlings, none over 14, who stood in front of the House and begged, pleaded and literally cried that they not be sent to the trenches of war. It was absolutely shocking. This side of the debate cared nothing for the issues of the amendment. They only wanted to use the sight of little girls and emotionalism to pierce hearts and control consciences. The sixth little girl told a story of how her brother would tie her up and leave her for hours. She was using it to illustrate that boys have more strength than girls. It seemed to me to be more about child abuse laws. She said that her mother always had to intervene and set her free. At that she introduced her mother who had allowed her bully brother to tie her up – Phyllis Schlafly, herself.

Phyllis stepped to the podium. She went on and on about these darling, fragile, porcelain young women who were the future mothers of Americans. She called upon the Representatives to not force them into the draft. She went on to say that the ERA would take women out of their homes, require unisex toilets, grant homosexuals favors, provide funding for abortions and force women into the trenches. How could this woman be an attorney? Does she really understand the law? Did she actually attend law school and pass the bar? She went on, "Women should stay home, admiring and appreciating their husbands and maintaining a happy disposition. The ERA threatens the superior stature that women currently have, mainly a husband who supports her, so she is free to follow her own interests."

Phyllis must be a very talented liar or she is severely addlepated. Where are all of these husbands who want to support their wives following their own interests? What is she saying about a woman raising three children, does she have any free time anyway? She also said that she believes that God is assisting her in the battle. This is not any God I want to know. Another Phyllisism: "The atomic bomb was a wise God's gift to a deserving America. Because God likes us better than anyone else, He will continue to help us build more atomic bombs than the Russians." Another: "When a woman walks across the room, she speaks with a universal body language that most men intuitively understand. Men hardly ever ask sexual favors of women when the certain answer is no."

Tuesday, June 8
Day 22

As we sat in the rotunda today a reporter came over to Sonia, knelt down, took out her pad and waited. Sonia paused a long time and said, "So, let's talk spaghetti." Everyone roared. She is so funny, even starving, she is funny.

No one would ever believe that the primary topic around here is food. Not just what we would like to eat, but cooking, menus and buffets. I expected the total opposite, that we would not want to hear a smidge about food. But it is food, food and, then, more food.

Mary's vinegar pie is getting as much air time as economic parity. Mary and Sonia actually bought some recipe books. They read them. They read them out loud. Yesterday I said that something might be as slick as a "knife through hot butter." Everyone moaned and began listing all the ways to use hot butter. All of our jokes, reading, TV, just driving down the street, conversation is filled with allusions to food. Dina is dreaming up a retail store that only carries popcorn. The flavors would be nationalities; Italian, Hawaiian, Mexican, etc.

A reporter brought me a bumper sticker that the Springfield police have on their cars, "They needed to lose weight anyway." I laughed. It was easier to laugh. I have always defended my size with jokes. But it really isn't funny. Today in the local paper, Phyllis was quoted saying, "Fasting is a good idea if you need to lose weight."

What are people thinking? Why do they talk about this in terms of vanity? Can a woman, risking her health and maybe even her life, be viewed and compared to some beauty contestant? Is she attractive? Is she in the Woman's Movement because she is ugly? One member of the Illinois House of Representatives said that we are nothing but, "brainless, braless broads." What are they talking about? Who are they talking to? Who is listening? Haven't they looked around and seen all of these articulate, brilliant, brave, inspiring women?

I just don't understand why weight is such an issue for women -- such an issue for me. It has always been factored into every decision, even when the outcome had nothing to do with size. I believe if you have fasted for twenty days for my rights, it is holy and respectful no matter what you weigh.

So they eat and we do not.

Today it is important.

We are hungry and they are not.

Tomorrow it will remain important.

Wednesday, June 9
Day 23

Win, lose or draw I will be home in three weeks.

Ellie Smeal and her troops came to the motel today. It was the second time this week. The talk is that, to get the heat off, the Senate will ratify and then the House will recess until July. When she told us, the wind went out of our sails. We had been hoping that if the House does recess, they will be forced back to a special session to vote before the deadline.

The Governor has the authority to do that. It would have two positive effects: 1) it will show the country Governor James R. Thompson's true position and 2) if there is a special session, they must vote on the rules change. Speaker Ryan would not be able to dodge the three-fifths issue.

If that is the actual scenario, we will move the fast from the rotunda to the Governor's office. That would put a spotlight on him and reveal his true position. He continually insists that he is pro-ERA but will not direct Speaker Ryan to introduce the rules change for a vote. As a matter of fact, they are running mates in the November elections.

To me it all feels like an irresolvable stalemate. Astrologically things do not look good. The moon has been void-of-course thirteen times in the twenty-three days we have been fasting. Energy is in constant ebb and flow, so it can't pick up momentum. Besides the moon being on and off course, FOUR planets are in retrograde. This is not good. I hope the energy will feel a bit more solid and stable as each retrograde planet go direct.

Mercury on the 13th.
Saturn on the 18th.
Jupiter on the 27th.
AND
Pluto doesn't go direct until July 4th.

Tonight J.R. and I went to see *Star Trek II*. What a disappointment. It was all just gore and guts. Where was Spock? I want to see a movie all about Vulcans.

People recognized us and followed us to our seats. They sat right behind us. It gives me the creeps.

Thursday, June 10
Day 24

Today is Maria's birthday. I love her so much. I am overwhelmed that I am here and she is not. I had buried deep in my wishing well that she would come here. She has not made any hint in that direction. She is high strung and has made it clear over the years that she does not want anything to do with the public or politics. I ordered flowers for her to be delivered today. I hope that they are perfect.

There are some lesbians here. Maybe I should qualify that by saying that there are lots of lesbians here but very few are out. Sonia has asked Dina and me to not confuse or distract focus on the ERA with sexual preference. I have no problem with that. People are already swamped with fears, projections, illusions about gender equality. Mixing that hodge podge with homosexuality is not necessary for me. I think we would end up having to explain how the issues are not related and be taken way off course. It is best to focus on the fact that traditional families will not be threatened by equal rights. So for today, we will stroll out the married mothers in green and white.

NOW has their problems with the issue of lesbianism. It has been made quite clear that the president of NOW cannot be a lesbian. At this point, it seems she has to be married as well. But I can't help but grieve over the loss of recognition for the many brilliant and brave lesbians who have dedicated their entire lives to the liberation of women -- all women, not just gay women.

While sitting in the rotunda today a reporter asked me if I had made any sense of it all. I think that is going to take a long time. There is just so much pain here. Everyone is feeling pain over this. I heard that Ellie is over-eating and others can't eat at all. And I see pain in the faces of the people who come and stare at us. They come and stand ten feet away from us and just stare. I remember Greg saying that they would do that, but it feels funny. Are we who they think we are?

I suppose this is exactly what we wanted to solicit but now that it is here, it is so sad and painful. Everyone seems so afraid. Are they afraid of losing? Are they afraid of winning? Do they think that the definition of "woman" will change? Who is this oppressor that actually lives inside of the oppressed?

I really feel lost. People parade by and tell me they love me. They don't even know me. They don't know that I love ice cream and poodles. I love books and hate rain and listen to classical music. I am so far left, that NOW can't see me.

And what about the people who say they hate me? They line up in front of us, with their children dressed in red and white, pointing at those evil fasters. There may be reasons to hate me, but fasting isn't one of them. What are they doing to their children? There are babies in strollers all decorated in red or green.

Why isn't this working? I am willing to die for equality and all I hear about is Robert's Rules of Order. What is the big deal? We aren't asking for equality in the kitchen, the bathroom or even the bedroom. No one could legislate that. All we want is to not be discriminated against in laws, insurance, employment, salaries, pensions and benefits. Why should anyone have to ask for these anyway?

I don't fit anywhere. When this is over, who will I be? I am starting to forget everything. All I am sure of is that I am not the person everyone is pointing at. I want to go home. I want to go home and never leave home again.

When can I go home and who will I be? I can only hope Maria will still love me.

Friday, June 11
Day 25

Thirteen women from the Grass Roots Group of Second Class Citizens went to the Governor's office today and blocked his doors. They tied themselves together with paper chains to avoid the injuries they got from the bolt cutters last week. Besides, the chains were very expensive and they lost all of them to the state police.

They simply sat on the floor and refused to budge. The police moved them to the sides and they returned, not once but twice. Then the third and final time they were moved, the police picked them up and carried them to the basement.

The House and Senate did not meet today, so we stayed at the motel. We decided that going to the Capitol when the legislatures are in session makes it clear that they and their vote are the focus of our fast. There was some wild talk about going to the Governor's mansion and sitting on his lawn. Doing so would not only shift attention to a non-voting person but it would surely land us in jail. The worse thing that could happen is for us to be out of sight.

So we hung around the motel. It is so cold out that most of us are freezing. We have complained to the motel a hundred times and asked them to turn off the air conditioning that is blowing in our rooms. As a last resort, we have all taped cardboard over the vents.

Mary Barnes is really suffering. She is hypoglycemic and her blood sugar is dangerously off. She started drinking honey and lemon in her water. She feels terrible about it but the press has not considered it breaking the fast.

The State Journal-Register ran a story, "ERA Fasters Go To The Movies." We saw *E.T.* It was so clever, a new way to tell the Christ story; miracles and resurrection.

The story in the Washington Post is really a whopper. After spending a full two days with us, the reporter wrote that we have to be bathed by helpers. *People* magazine sent a reporter here for a few days too. I can't wait to see what they are going to say.

Maybe that is all we can do right now -- wait. Let the press parade through, look and report back to the world on what we are doing. What more could we do?

Although I would not complain out loud, I am surprised that more people didn't stay after last week's rally. Why isn't the Capitol filled with women from all over the country demanding their rights? What's the big deal? Pack a bag, kiss the family, take off for the State Capital of your choice.

You don't have to fast.

Just show up.

Saturday, June 12
Day 26

Another day with nothing to do. All to look forward to is the mail. We have gotten bags and bags of it. We keep one big box of general mail that I am organizing. I thought I would copy a few of them into my journal.

Dear Zoe Ann,
I am fully committed to the issue of equal rights under the law. But you must be out of your mind to ask for Phyllis Shlafly's autograph. Does campaigning for injustice to women make her a celebrity in your eyes? Well not in mine. Why not wear a button that says, "Stop Shlafly!"
Sincerely,
Audrey Tjepkeme

Dear Sonia, Maureen, Zoe Ann, Dina, Mary, Shirley and MaryAnn,
Because I am expecting a baby any day now, I have decided to not join you in your fast for the ratification of the ERA. However I would like to commend you for your courage and dedication to a cause that will make all citizens equal. I would like to offer you encouragement and hope and, most of all, a heartfelt thank you for acting on the wishes of a majority of Americans and risking your health for ratification in Illinois. I watch the national news anxious to hear about you, hoping fervently that your fast will not be in vain and the Governor Thompson and the legislators will change the majority rule. You have my whole hearted support.
Karen Dunning

Do you realize how completely silly you are acting, fasting and chained?
If your kids did this sort of thing you'd wollup them but good. Here's a
whammy on the fannies of each of you.
Go Home and get some sleep.
ERA stands for The Equal Rights Amendment.

Dear Sonia Johnson,
I have been telling my little friend Heather about the ERA. She thinks it's
a good idea. She is my best friend at school. Thank you.
Love,
Heidi
age 9, Third Grade

We support your cause. Unequivocally.
However we need you healthy, productive and with us.
Please stop your fast.
Nurses at the Evanston Hospital
Evanston, Illinois

Dear Sonia and Her Seven Sisters,
I am a disabled woman who heard of you and your fight which is my fight
too and I want to tell you I love you. I send you strength and energy. Soon,
when you emerge victorious for all women, you may wish to come and
have some rest and relaxation at the Beechtree, 21 acres of womyn's land
where I live. I am a very good cook and would be honored to make dinner
from vegetables that will be grown in our garden. Your hunger feeds the
hearts of many.
Love in sisterhood,
Coretta.

Dear Women,
I read about what you are doing tonight in the papers and it brought tears
to me eyes. I am so proud that there are women like you. What you are
doing is wonderful and will have a great effect on other women. Don't let
anyone give you a hard time. They are stupid and stupid people are what
got us into this mess in the first place.
More power to you! I don't pray, but my good thoughts are with you, if
that means anything.
Love,
Joanne Halatali

PS My son Andrew says he would like to go to the hospital and block your view of anyone who is eating a big dinner.

HUNDREDS MARCH NUDE -- - -- FOR ERA
"Hundreds of nude women packed legislative galleries, blocked hallways and marched in street of Springfield, Oklahoma City, Tallahassee and Raleigh - - insisting on ERA ratification."
  Neither the legislators or police will know how to deal with hundreds of nude women. Very wide news coverage of such a demonstration will place intense pressure on legislators to pass ERA.
  Without a lot of fresh publicity, ERA won't pass. Chains and hunger strikes, no longer fresh news. Large nude marches will be the number one headline for days on all TV, radio and newspapers. To purchase such publicity, would cost millions.

To the Fasting Women,
  I just had to write and tell you my opinion of what you are doing. First of all, it is just plain blackmail and I sure hope that our Senators and Representatives will not be swayed by that.
  Secondly, I think it is a shame (and probably a waste of taxpayer's money) that the doctors in Springfield have to spend their time trying to save your lives when you are absolutely doing this to your own bodies.
  Thirdly, there just may be some points to ERA (but if you can't get votes for it in the right way, why try to starve yourselves to death?). BUT women in the United States can have a good life. I know because I live here and I love it!
  I also heard this morning that Vice-president Bush will not stop to see you. I am glad that he doesn't recognize you by making that effort. You have the right to work for the ERA (that's the good part about this country) but you are sure going about it in the wrong way!
A "happy to be a woman" woman who doesn't need ERA,
Mrs. George Meseke

Priests for Equality
Hyattsville, MD 20782

To: Zoe Ann Ananda, Dina Bachelor, Mary Barnes, Mary Ann Beall, Sonia Johnson, Shirley Wallace, and Maureen Fiedler RSM,

On behalf of the Board of Directors of Priests for Equality, I am writing to express our deep support and solidarity with you during your sacrificial fast for justice and equality.

The issue of equality for women in this country has taken much sacrifice, devotion and commitment of life and energies of many noble women throughout the century. The seven of you stand in a long historical tradition of Feminist struggle and resistance to the forces of patriarchy; which have, for too long, dominated the social, political and economic life of this nation.

The Equal Rights Amendment is the minimum commitment this country needs to make the cause of equality for women and men. As an organization that speaks on behalf of over 1800 Roman Catholic priests, we call upon all religious persons, and in particular, the leaders of the various churches to give active support for the passage of the E.R.A. in this last month for ratification.

We are with you, sisters, in this struggle. We pledge to speak for the ratification from the pulpits in this last month as many of our members have done over the last seven years. We pledge to continue our struggle with the male dominated hierarchy and structures for the Roman Catholic Church so that Catholic women will have access to the same ministries, office and responsibilities that men presently have. We pledge our prayers to the loving Mother/Father God that your lives and health may be preserved during this fast and that hardened hearts may be moved by your action to give active support for passage of the Equal Rights Amendment by June 30. Finally, as proof of our love and solidarity with your sacrificial action, each of the eleven members of the Priests for Equality Board of Directors is committed to fast each Wednesday of the month of June.

In sister/brotherhood,

Brother Joseph Izzo C.F.X.
National Secretary, Priests for Equality

Dear Fasters,

I appreciate your dedication and willingness to risk your health in order to grab public attention and force them to rethink the seriousness of the ERA. Please take care of yourselves as best you can. I am a M.D. at the Cook County Hospital in Chicago. I am still in training but am somewhat familiar with the disturbances your body may go through without nutrition. Please be careful. I would hate to have you suffer undo harm or lose your life because of inadequate monitoring of simple electrolytes or metabolic disturbances prior to the time pure starvation alone will have its effect.

We are all here today in Springfield to show our support of you and the ERA. It is one of our last big "hurrahs" before the public, before the deadline of June 30.

Love to you all and victory for all womankind,
Maureen Ruder

Sunday, June 13
Day 27

If I were *Queen for a Day*, I would invent a new world. It would be a world of women living as women are meant to live. It would be a matriarchy and it would be heavenly.

All relationships would be limitless and feelings would be infinite. There would be no worry about running out of love. One would not have to deny a feeling or a relationship to prevent jealousy or protect possessiveness.

Among the highest values would be difference. If anyone was afraid of difference, they would learn to transform that fear into love because fear can only lead to oppression and pain. We would love difference. We would nurture and celebrate difference. Books, movies, even schools would promote and reward difference. It would be such a grand treasure that tolerance would not even be necessary.

In my world, pretend would precede real. One would only have to believe to make it happen. All we would have to do is live our lives without attachment to the result. Manipulation would disappear. Love would carry no expectation.

It would unfold just like a flower in time-lapse photography. Even in death the flowers and trees go to seed and give birth again. Yin would unfold, never beginning, never ending, always in motion, expanding, contracting. The only constant would be evolution.

There would be no exploitation. There would be no need for it. Ownership, walls, limits, hierarchy, linear thinking would atrophy and fade away. Dancing would be two equals, sharing the floor, whistling the music. Both dancers would know their role and give themselves to it completely.

So Jack Bailey, where are you when I need you? It is a simple request. Here is a story the audience will love. Oppression and hardship would be met head on. Crown me *Queen for a Day* before June 30.

But in the meantime, all I can do is try to make it happen on my own. I must try to lift the patriarchal grid from my own experience and live as if I am *Queen for a Day*. I must refuse to dance the patriarchal dance and if they won't let me on their dance floor then I will have a secret one of my own inside.

The innocence and purity of my own spirit must live a secret life dancing in protected spaces. In homes across the country, women dance a secret dance forming their own liberation and freedom. On the streets and in the work place women may appear that they are satisfied and cooperative but, in their hearts, they are learning to be free.

They are a band of spiritual midwives weaving a web of light and freedom. Their lives are dedicated to healing what has gone on before. There will be hurts. Hurts are unavoidable and we must not avoid the hurts, as they can heal.

I am so fortunate to be able to live an open life. No one can fire me or require me to be their projection. Here in Springfield I am able to demonstrate my hopes and dreams. I must never stop believing in this possibility. I read that Helen Caldicott said that it would be better to go down on the side of right than to step away from the conflict. We just have to believe in the intent, detach from the outcome and embrace the task that is directly in front of us. Everyone of us must spend everything we have to make this dream come true.

I am the Queen of hope. There is nothing but hope. There is hope because I can make my dream come true. I can change right this very minute. I can be peaceful. I have equality in my life. I cannot wait for laws. I cannot wait for crowds. I cannot wait for anything. My awareness requires simultaneous action. No committee, no House, no Senate, no vote. I declare my personal Constitution does not need an amendment, it includes and is based on equality.

Maybe that is what I am learning here in Springfield, Illinois. Maybe I am finding out that a law cannot be written until its essence unfolds within a human heart. I had thought that legislators would draw in evolution and vote it into the social consciousness. Now I am considering that evolution occurs within an individual's heart. Nothing more to wait for.

How I live will be my blueprint for the future.

Monday, June 14
Day 28

This morning we held a press conference. Every time we go into the pressroom there are more people than the time before. It is as if they are waiting for us to say something surprising. There is a lot of anxiety and anticipation. Maybe they are waiting for us to give up and end the fast.

WOMEN FASTING FOR THE EQUAL RIGHTS AMENDEMENT
URGE VICE-PRESIDENT BUSH
TO MEET THEM IN SPRINGFIELD.

The seven women fasting for ratification of the Equal Rights Amendment today sent a telegram to Vice-President George Bush:

Dear Vice-President Bush,
    Several days ago you actively joined in witness to the truth, justice and power of fasting for the cause of human rights by meeting with Lois Becker Frolova who was fasting to release her husband from the Soviet Union. Your meeting contributed to freedom for her husband and the reunion of that family.
    With that same spirit and hope for freedom, we urge you to meet with us in Springfield, Illinois prior to June 20. We are the seven women who began a solemn fast here 28 days ago to witness to women's deep hunger for

justice and to call for speedy ratification of the Equal Rights Amendment. We, representing the majority of U.S. citizens, need your intervention even more desperately than did Lois Becker Frolova. There are 16 days left to ratify this amendment. Clearly, our country – which purports to stand for human rights within its borders.

Though this is a perilous hour for the Equal Rights Amendment and for women, it is also a perilous hour for the Republican Party. As the highest ranking Republican favoring the Equal Rights Amendment, you alone may be able to save your party from a permanent "anti-woman" stigma and from massive defeats in the 1982 elections. Therefore, we urge you to meet not only with us, but with Governor Thompson, Speaker Ryan and other Republican leaders in Illinois as well, persuading them to use every available resource and all the power at their command to achieve ratification. Your intervention at this hour could well move Illinois and the nation toward fulfilling the 200-year-old promise of full equal human rights under the law.

We await your arrival,

Zoe Ann Ananda   Sr. Maureen Fiedler
Dina Bachelor   Dr. Sonia Johnson
Mary Barnes   Shirley Wallace
Mary Ann Beall

ADDRESS:
Ramada Inn
3751 South 6th Street
Springfield, Illinois 62703
(217) 529-5511

Afterwards we went to the rotunda and it was particularly slow. The cold marble floor, second and third floor balconies are empty and lifeless. Where is everyone? Where is NOW? Where is the ACLU? Where are all of the people? Where are all of the women? Where is every mother with their daughters? There is a sense that things are over. We have come to this place, this moment with full anticipation of being included in the Constitution and today, for the first time, I have to consider that we may not get it.

What will life be like if we don't get it? Everything I have done thus far in the Women's Movement has been in preparation of success. I have lectured and put up with countless insults. I have stood toe to toe with the anti-feminists and opened my heart to them. I endured their jokes, tolerated their blatant sexism and explained a thousand times what this amendment is about, but now I realize I did all of it believing in success.

How would I have behaved if I had known it would fail? Would I have taken it in stride? Would I have held my temper and tried so hard to explain why men and women are not meant to be in positions of master and servant. Women are not confined to mothering and destined to fail if they leave the kitchen. And if they believe that women are less intelligent, does that mean mothering doesn't require intelligence?

The story in today's *TIME* magazine says that it is all over. What will it feel like when I go home without the amendment?

Tuesday, June 15
Day 29

Most Venerable Mohandas K. Gandhi,

Are you here with me? I love you more than anyone living
or dead, so you must be here with me. If your spirit answers
all who call on your teachings for social change on behalf of
liberation, then you are here.

Many times I have imagined being alive at the same time
as you. I would have traveled to India to be near you, to work
with you. Better yet, maybe in my last life I was near you. I
was born eight months after you were killed. I would have
lived at the ashram and spun and walked and listened.

In any event, Ahimsa lives in my heart. Those ideals live
above, below, around and within each of us, in the best parts
of us. I know you reached with courage, stillness and resolve,
so they would be available to you. It may be breaking my
heart, but I can't seem to connect with them here.

It is 1982 and I am a satyagrahi living in the United
States. My principles are that of Ahimsa and my subject is the
liberation of women. I am using my life to change the hearts
of law makers. I am refusing to participate in their unjust
system. I am making my choices visible. I am offering my life

to irresistibly demonstrate the truth so they will be unable
to hold their position as it is without conscience, without
truth, without love. Here we are fighting a different battle in
a different culture, at different time. My issues are not your
issues. My concerns are not your concerns. My goals are not
your goals. But I have deeply considered, deeply believed and
deeply embraced non-cooperation, Satyagraha and Ahimsa.

Have I been wrong to hope these teachings are timeless?
Did it take weeks of not eating and facing the public response
to finally get it? And, I have to say, I am not a push-over on
this. The dreamer in me does not require social approval or
immediate results. So let's look together. I can look, if we look
together. I am worried that the oppression of women is too
old, too embedded to ever be unveiled, stand unvarnished and
attract scrutiny. In your journey, the British had been in India
for 250 years and the ancient soul of India was intact. Millions
of Indians knew that essentially the country belonged to them
and not the British.

The issues I am confronting are centuries old, accepted
and completely integrated into my society. They are not just
familiar, but widely accepted. In fact women vote on, rely
on and support the very laws that oppress them. As always
women pledge their lives for their families, but now it often
means being the family's sole provider, working for fifty-nine
cents on the dollar, being sexually harassed and discriminated
against. Sadly, for a woman to put herself second is familiar,
expected and, often, falsely elevated.

Gandhiji, it seems that my opponent is impossible to
embarrass. Surely the British knew that they went too far
with the massacre of Amritsar. The mistreatment of Indians
was unmistakable. Here, men are not embarrassed at all
about the treatment of women. In fact, they celebrate it in
their institutions, their laws and their arts. Men have agreed
to harass women, beat women, rape women, desert women
and to support one another's right to do so. Is my culture
so dispassionate that we cannot ever embarrass them to a

position of sympathy?

I am afraid that assuming a posture of humility and service, as you did Gandhi, will only play into the hands of the oppressors here. You were a man and demonstrating humility and self-sacrifice shocked your opponents. But women have bowed their heads for centuries, raising them only to see men through times of poverty or war.

With each passing year and each victory, national Indian support was building in information, participation and spirit. Every Indian who had not been co-opted by the British wanted them to leave. However, here in the U.S., we don't want the oppressor to "walk out." We want them to stop the oppression and live with us as equals. The British would never have relinquished their privileges to live as equals with Indians.

Was I wrong when I thought this fast would make a difference? Your fasts happened after years of international fame and honored political work. You were sixty-three when you fasted to end the violence between Muslims and Hindus. You were the "Father of India," the conscience of India and her population watched and adored your every move. Here there are no long standing heroines whose sacrifice or death would mobilize the nation. We seven women are really no one in particular, only all women in general.

As hard as the British tried to convince the Indians that they were not full citizens, an ancient and proud history made that impossible. American women have only known lives as second class citizens. The laws, the institutions, the fabric of society reflect and maintain the unequal status of the genders. This imbalance is accepted by most citizens -- male and female. The culture states it clearly -- just go to any museum, any library, any bookstore and ask for the women's section.

When you and other resisters went to prison, the Indian people found it to be a source of pride and inspiration. Here, women do not believe that they are worth fasting for, certainly

not going to jail for. The press agrees and, I am sorry to
say, so do many of the family and friends of women who are
resisting with me today. We have gotten letters asking us
to stop, saying that we are hysterical and that the issue is
not worth the sacrifice. Oddly it is important and respected
when a woman fasts for men's rights. Vice-President Bush
recently commended and assisted a woman who fasted for the
liberation of her husband.

I know that you were an educated and privileged man. You
gave up your position when it served your purposes. And you
had a devoted spouse who could stay home and care for your
children. When you gave up the right to a legal defense, it was
a gesture, as you yourself had been called to the bar and were
fully capable of legally defending yourself. You had economic
supporters who built ashrams, sustained communities and
published your writings. You had warned Indians that the
worst thing they could do was adopt the ways of the British
and that it would never bring them the power they wanted. So,
you wove cloth, wore a dhoti and identified with the poor. But
in the U.S., women are already poorer than men. We have no
ashram, no community, no group support. We sit here with no
idea where any money is coming from. We have not worked for
weeks, have no income and no tickets to get home when this
ends. We have no rich benefactors. In fact, most of us have
challenged job security even further by publicly demanding
equal wages and benefits.

I have to face that for you, Ahimsa is rooted in the
spirit. Your soul, informed by your beliefs, directed your
life. Satyagraha is based in prayer and the satyagrahi relies
on God for protection from the oppressor's brute force. You
had a spiritual system within the political movement and a
political movement within a spiritual system. People believed
that it was their dharma to fight British rule. Each act of
civil disobedience was seen as a religious action performed to
advance, educate and enlighten all of humanity. Here we are

seen as godless. We are seen as irreverent. We are even seen as evil.

In your culture, God is both male and female, Mother and Father. Tolerance is part of your religious practice. And here, if we continue to make religion a matter of scripture and teachings only, then we are forever lost. Be it Christianity or Judaism or any other religion practiced by a large number of Americans, it is imbued with gender inequity. I need women to see that true spirituality is a matter of the heart. Women's hearts are always spilling over with courage and love. We just need to see ourselves as worthy recipients. Will women ever think enough of themselves to have living heroines? To go to jail? To fast or even die for women's rights? I don't want women to adopt men's ways of waiting for their heroes to die before honoring them. We need living heroines. We need to find that supporting them is a form of participation. I want women to embrace this movement as their dharma.

I am sad in peeling off my blinders about you. You are my beloved, but it seems you cannot be the hero of my movement. I cannot take your teachings and translate them to meet my needs, like a seamstress altering a coat. I love your simplicity and humility and your pace that never rode thoughtlessly over anyone. In your seventy-nine years you offered me a hope of a world gone sane.

But maybe there is a freedom in my discovery. We must be our own heroines. We must not be held back by the past. We must fly in the face of necessity and be our own greatest inspiration. We must step up and claim our rights. The goal here is not to throw ourselves further into economic hardship but to be skilled, reliant, resourceful. Women must begin to prefer their independence, not just recover from being abandoned.

The Hungry Heart

The one thing I will not give up between us is that I love you. You honored your soul and I need to do that too. I don't want to ever think of myself as disposable as the oppressor would have me believe. I am my own greatest resource. I am a creation of Woman Spirit.

So where does that leave us? I have an inkling that you and I will leave here even closer. I am discovering an inner liberation that I never considered before. I don't think I will ever be scared into silence again. They can never demand or receive obedience from me. They can no longer require me to abandon myself. I have found my own source. I have discovered more courage than I ever expected. I have loved and respected myself. The oppressor has lost me forever.

Goodbye, Gandhiji. You have set me free. You fed me, nurtured me, inspired me. Now you must say goodbye. I will be on my way. The circle is complete between us. I must be my own heroine.

Wednesday, June 16
Day 30

In two weeks I will be home. Will I have equality? Will I bring home equality? Will equality become law? And how will anyone demonstrate this newly won equality? Will the grocery store be any different? The high school? The nearest church? Even this generation of children? The fact is, at this point, I don't even care. All I care about is getting home. I want to go home. I want to be with Maria and my poodle Licky and not here. I fall asleep every night thinking about my flight home; what I will wear, what I will do and, most of all, what I will eat.

Everyone here is in terrible pain that never lets up. J.R. says it isn't actually pain. It is a deep and suffocating sadness. All of us live just on the cliff of weeping. My vulnerability is higher than I have ever consciously maintained. Today Sonia got mad at me in the rotunda about a letter I was passing down the row to Mary Ann. Two weeks ago, it would not have mattered to any of us. But now, between no food and eroding hope about our cause, it was more than I could handle and I cried out loud, right then and there. I am sorry I cried. I think it made the other fasters feel bad. Until now, I have been the strong one, the controlled one, the sturdy one. I feel as if I took that away from them.

The Hungry Heart

The NOW guard was particularly attentive. They are always near us. They stand in front and behind us. I am not used to being touched by people I don't know very well. I had told them weeks ago that I didn't like all of the hugging that was going on. It just isn't something I am comfortable with – never have been. But this morning Judy and Vicki told all of us that they decided, when they met last night, that we needed to be touched. So all day one of the guards was behind each of us twiddling with our hair or rubbing our shoulders. Secretly I wonder if they know something they have not told us. Is there a certain danger brewing? Or are they only trying to keep us grounded?

Nonetheless I am stirred and tenderized by the support of the NOW guard. Judy, Vicki, Kathy and Louise are more overtly and freely loving than any women I have ever known. I have held them at a distance until today, just as I would any strangers, but now they are so close and so vital, they are irresistible. I feed on their inner strength. I drink in their resolve. I am sustained by their spirit. They fill me up.

It is beginning to feel as if we are an intimate tribe. Today they treated me as if I was a member of a close, loving, kind and informed family. They behaved in ways that I have only read about but never believed. I have read a dozen books about groups of women being openly affectionate, caring for one another above all else. Frankly, I thought it was merely romanticizing the past by portraying the Nineteenth and early Twentieth Century lesbians as living in private, sensual and intimate circles.

Today was erotic and intimate and open and generous. It was both natural and foreign. It was intoxicating and more attractive than I can explain. It presented a familiarity that, while being sexual, includes respect for everyone's lifemates and commitments. They kiss, they hug, they listen, they share at a depth that, up until this event, I had only known in my primary relationship. I see why all other relationships appeared flat. They were flat. They were unnecessarily flat. This group of women deepened the possibility of human intimacy for me and I doubt if they would ever guess it.

Tonight, upon reflection, it feels as if I have stepped into the world I want to live in. This is the matriarchy as I have idealized it. It is an intimate, unguarded circle of women who are clear about defining their own relationships and find no threat in being present, available, physical and generous. Single women would be safe. Coupled women would be safe. Children would be safe. In fact, men would be safe. Whatever configuration of relationship a person may choose, it would be regarded, respected and unquestioned.

This is not the Michigan Women's Music Festival. This is not NOW. This is not a vacation or clubs or bars. This is my literary, spiritual and unspoken ideal. This is not what I am fasting for. I am fasting for equality of rights under the law in the U.S. I am fasting to legislate treating adults without regard to gender. I am fasting to criminalize discrimination. But my heart wants so much more.

I want a life built on trusting, intimate and integrated relationships. I want humans to meet without judgment, to join without conditions, to not require safeguards. I want danger and oppression relegated to fiction. I want limitless welcome, boundless potential and open communication. I want food for the body and the mind and soul to be equally important.

The timing of this great gift was miraculous. I thank god that they made the choices they did last night because the rotunda was a mad house at noon today. There must have been two thousand people assembled for a pro-ERA rally. It was mostly the United Auto Workers and the Illinois Teachers Association. Kristen Lems gave a concert and there were a few speakers. One of them was Catherine, a thirteen year old young woman from Chicago. She said that everyday after school she worked as a volunteer at her local NOW office. She came to Springfield to personally talk with her State Senator. He told her that he did not care about re-election so he was definitely voting against the ERA. Then he said that she is a pretty little girl and should not be concerned about such things. Catherine told him that she didn't care to stand on his pedestal or anyone else's.

For the most part I just sit on my folding chair and write letters. I try to use it as a means of insulation. When I look up I see groups of people just staring. They whisper. They jeer. They marvel. They are hateful or humbled. To me it feels like they are sucking the life right out of me. In the beginning of the fast, it was all so exciting, the people in the rotunda were energizing, but now it feel like a wake and we are the focus of the mourners. One woman walked right up to us, stood in front of each of us and said that she just wanted to look into our eyes. I hated that! What was she doing?

The New York Times ran a quotation today from Bush's office, "The Vice President supported the original amendment. But he personally did not support the extension and the Reagan administration does not support the ERA. He does not get involved in anything against the platform." So that cuts us loose from three hours of meetings, letter writing and issuing another press release. Vice-President Bush is off the hook and not an advocate anymore.

Yesterday twelve women from the Grass Roots Group of Second Class Citizens worked their way into the House. There were lots of people waiting outside of the chambers as it was lobby day for the UAW and several other groups. Strategically the chainers waited in the crowd for their chance to slip in. When a legislator opened the door and invited in a group of lobbyists, they moved in right behind them, went to the front of the floor, laid down and refused to move. It must have been quite a scene. I wish I could have seen it. In the midst of the ruckus Representative James Kelley of Rockford, who weighs over 300 pounds, stomped on two of the women. They are both on crutches today. They plan to sue.

We had a long tedious planning meeting tonight. We have to face that there is a nationwide move to block the ERA. The word from Florida is very grim. We had been considering sending some of the fasters to Tallahassee but that just isn't practical. Talk has begun about ending the fast and leaving Illinois. What are the criteria for staying? We never really talked about it. Are we obligated to NOW? Just to be on the safe side, Dina has made flight reservations to Los Angeles for J.R., herself and me on June 24, 26, 29 and July 2. The east coast women are going to the July 1st Washington D.C. rally. They want to be eating as soon as possible to collect strength so they can partake in any civil disobedience that might happen there.

We talked about the chainers too. Some of the women here think that the chainers disrupting the floor may increase the chances for adjournment until after the June 30th deadline. Hell, if it is all over, why not? I don't care. I just want them to be unforgettably outrageous. They are creating history. They are creating my history. We are creating our history. It better be something worth remembering.

Thursday, June 17
Day 31

I am writing this while waiting for a meeting to start in Dixie's room. It is going to be some meeting! We are expecting all of the principals of this drama to arrive shortly.

We just got some terrible news about the motel. They have booked a convention and every room is reserved and paid for as of June 25. They say there is nothing they can do about it. That is a full week away and I just cannot handle thinking about it. Our security, privacy, sleeping and bathing conditions are the only solid ground we have. I will worry about it on the 24th.

One topic that keeps on floating to the surface is sending some of us to Oklahoma. Oh my god. I know that I can't orient myself to another place – new faces, new places and even less privacy. We have got to get this thing over with. Somebody needs to say out loud that we have not eaten in thirty-one days. Please I just want someone to say it out loud and express genuine worry. I think we should have a press conference, end the fast and go home. We came here to fast for the ERA. The ERA is never going to pass, so why are we still fasting?

The Hungry Heart

I see J.R. with her diet soda and cigarettes. I want a diet 7UP. The machine is right outside my door and all night long I hear people throwing in their quarters. In the lobby, just to the left of the door is a candy machine. I pass it everyday when I get the mail for us. The very minute the fast is over, I am going to buy a Three Musketeers Bar. There is a place we drive past every day that sells frozen yogurt. They make a different flavor everyday and post the flavor de jour on a big sandwich sign on the sidewalk. I hope I can get there too.

On Tuesday, June 22, if the fast is still going, a group of Catholics will be joining us for the day. Now there's a bit of irony. Maybe there is someone out there who will be impressed, but it certainly is not me. I would be impressed by a thousand women storming the Capitol. I would be very impressed if five thousand women descended on Springfield and refused to leave the Capitol without the ERA. I would be impressed if fifty thousand women simply showed up!

But anyway, the Catholics are coming for a one day fast. Okay, so I have not eaten in thirty-one days and they had an egg McMuffin on the way to the Capitol. I am very impressed with one of the Catholics who is coming, Sister Theresa Kane. She stood up in public and said a few words to the Pope. She is the head of the largest order of American nuns, The Sisters of Mercy of the Union. She urged His Holiness to consider including women in the ministry and the liturgy. She asked that the definition of God include both male and female. I know there are many wonderful women in religious orders, but why they continue giving their obedience to the Pope is beyond my understanding. Anti-abortion, anti-birth control, anti-women in the ministry; this man does not deserve any woman's obedience.

Just this minute the NOW women arrived: Ellie Smeal, Alice Cohan, Judy Block, Kathy Samer and Vicki Fuergeson. With them are a few members of the Grassroots Group of Second Class Citizens: Sue Yarber, Mary Lee Sargent, and Kari Alice Lynn.

Next week there will be a summit meeting in Chicago. It seems that Governor Thompson is in a bind. He has publicly stated that he is pro-choice and pro-women's rights. He has told the press that it is the Democrats who are delaying the ERA. His plan is to kill the ERA in the Senate and take off the pressure. The rumor is that he is twenty points behind Stevenson. NOW wants to force the vote in the House first and make sure the pressure continues.

The GGSCC has come here to discuss any and all concerns or suggestions that we might be able to offer. NOW believes that since the doorkeepers work for Speaker Ryan, they actually let the chainers into the House yesterday. Ellie and Alice are telling us that Speaker Ryan had intentionally called for lighter security and purposely arranged the day's schedule to include debating pro-women bills. While the GGSCC were lying on the floor in protest, the usually hot tempered Speaker Ryan was cool and controlled. Every bill that was on the docket concerned the welfare of women and children. Erv Kupcinet, of Channel 2 in Chicago, said that he found out that the Sergeant of Arms had been ordered to step aside and deliberately let the women in at that time.

So now we are being told that the entire thing is actually staged. When there is a vote, all of the Stop-ERA troops will be out on a grand scale. They come to session wearing suits and ties with red and white flowers on their desks. When there isn't a relevant vote, they are in white shirt sleeves and casual. It does seem odd that Phyllis Schlafly and all of her Eagle Forum friends turn out when there is a vote. They have advance notice. Duh.

In the rotunda today we were all harassed. It is a low key, extremely intense and relentless irritation. Two or three anti's will stand near us and just stare. They line up children and tell them that we are witches. Bit by bit, they are closing in on us. The NOW guard has noticed that it is getting harder to keep people at a safe distance. People step on our feet and crush into us as they get on the elevator. One thing that really seems weird is that Phyllis has asked for more security in the rotunda. No one would hurt her.

They want to defeat the ERA and malign us in the mix. They want the women in the movement to look as bad as possible. They want the pro-ERA people to appear responsible for the defeat. We don't have the energy to even think about such intrigue. They must have a lot of free time. They certainly have energy and focus.

Some people are concerned about depression and misplaced anger. Could there be suicides? Could some women just shut the door and resign from life? There are so many who have sacrificed everything for this. Women have left home and asked their families to be patient. Millions of hours on the phone, millions of flyers, millions of buttons and bumper stickers and hopes and dreams for equality. Kitchens and dining room tables have been buzzing over this for such a long time.

We are just days away from this being over and what will happen? What will happen to the structures that have been created to support this? Combining the three years with the three month extension, this is the longest amendment campaign ever waged. This is not a simple notion. This is not a road tax bill. This is a defining factor for millions of women and men who believe that laws set the standard for society. While we all know that the passage of the Equal Rights Amendment would not mean true or instant equality, its failure would make the inequality unbearable.

Friday, June 18
Day 32

Dear God,

Please help me. Please help me figure out what I am
supposed to do. Please help me understand who I am in this. I
am lost. The ERA is lost. I have lost it.

I tried. I tried my very best. Is it my fault? I realize that
I am only one woman and I never could have done it alone. I
know that I am not solely responsible, but has Woman failed?
Was it really not Her time?

In the avalanche of letters, dollars, lobbying, votes and
intentions, sit seven women. Why did we come here and
what purpose have we served? People parade by and throw
their feelings at us. We are like a Rodin in a gallery of living
art. There are no personalities here. Who knows the heart or
soul of an artist's model? Who knows the heart of the artist?
And in the end, does it matter? Caravaggio was accused of
murdering several people -- were his paintings less inspired,
less inspiring? Were our hearts not pure enough to turn the
hearts of the opponents?

I remember going to the Wisconsin State Fair and paying to
see the biggest woman in the world. Admission was a dollar.

Behind a curtain was a long house trailer with one entire wall of two way glass. When I walked behind the curtain, I found her sitting on a couch. She was so sad. I was so sad. I wanted the glass to be lifted up. I wanted to sit on the couch with her and she with me. I wanted all of the differences that I had paid to see to go away. "I am big, too," I wanted to tell her.

Am I in the glass trailer now? Is the rotunda my glass trailer? They look at me and I look at them. Are we so separate? They have rights and I do not. I have a relentless desire to change things and they want things to stay the same. Maybe all we have in common is the passion. But even when I pause and admire their devotion, I don't feel a hint of their respect in return.

We are hostages of a movement. We have been called from our homes and families to be a symbol. Just as the hostages in Iran became emblems of the U.S. or astronauts became human flags hurling through space, we are the ERA to some people. They stand in front of us and speak of their feelings about women, as if we cannot hear them, as if we have no ears connected to hearts. My exterior has become the ERA and I am lost. The ERA is lost.

If the ERA is my lover, I am standing over her deathbed now. There is nothing I can do for her now. We were mad passionate lovers. We danced to many a tune and laughed through many a night. You brought me true and lasting sisters. Our family has grown so. But now you are dying and there is nothing I can do. We had such plans, you and I. We were going to change the face of the earth, you and I. Women were going to be included in the Constitution and it was just the beginning.

Please, dear God, what shall we do now?
The ERA is lost and so am I.

Saturday, June 19
Day 33

I woke up this morning to the news that Mary Ann was taken to the hospital last night. One of her lungs partially collapsed. I remember when we first arrived in Springfield there was some concern because Mary Ann had just gotten over a bout of pneumonia. She had chest pain all day yesterday. It was so bad that Mary Ann, in her quiet Quaker way, let it be known that she was in trouble. She said that at this point she does not intend to break the fast.

I imagine most people will never understand her decision. They think since the amendment has not passed, the fast is moot. People can't stop calling this a hunger strike. I am shocked that no matter how many times and in how many ways we tell them otherwise, people think this is a hunger strike. This is not and has never been about bribery. We do not want to bribe the Illinois Legislature. THIS IS A PRAYER!! Please somebody hear me -- this is a prayer. We are praying to change voters' hearts and, thus, their votes. Mary Ann continuing through her illness is deepening her prayer.

Something really odd happened in the rotunda yesterday. Shirley's two sons arrived for a visit. One was wearing a Pro-ERA button and the other with a STOP-ERA button. I know they are both her sons, but we are hanging on a thread here about anything red and white. Not having eaten in thirty-three days, about all any of us can manage is "Green & White is safe," and "Red & White is danger." Now, with Shirley's anti-ERA son, a Red & White has free access within our guards' circle. All of the other anti-ERA people have no idea who he is and want to know why they can't get so close. Why are we being friendly with him? And the press is going to really use this one. I think that when inside of our area or in public, he needs to take off the button.

I was rude. I admit it. I simply didn't want him to suddenly be a part of our entourage. I don't want to be around people who think we are crazy and wrong. I don't want to be confronted and prodded, not now, not day thirty-three. Maureen was put off too. We all had words and, unfortunately, the press was eating up all of it. I wish we could have talked about it in private before the boys arrived. That would have been the correct way to treat the group. Maybe we could have put our heads together and issued a press statement. Maybe we could have turned it in a positive direction. But now the media is reporting that there is a rift between us and that is not true. The local paper ran a whole piece about it.

It's funny. Had I known that they were coming I might have really thought it through. What do you do when someone you love is actively opposed to your views? It can't be as easy as cutting them out of your life. My immediate reaction is unmitigated intolerance but I think that is coming from my state of fasting. Given some nutrition and time, matters of the heart are never black and white, green and white or red and white.

I just can't imagine the complexity of a mother's love. How do you love unconditionally when a child has become your adversary? Becomes dangerous? Becomes what you have always identified as immoral? During the Viet Nam War, I decided that I would never have children. My husband wanted kids, but I knew that I could not risk having a son who served in the military. I knew that I could not be a parent; that sacred relationship must never include conditions or expectations. I think it is better to not have kids at all than take such a risk. Maybe I am completely wrong. Maybe once a person has a child they discover a whole new type of love, but I have never seen it.

I hope Shirley knows I am sorry that I hurt her feelings. I am glad I don't have that kind of heartbreak in my life. She must be very torn.

We started today with a meeting at 11 A.M. Feelings are a bit tense but things will iron out. We listened to a tape of Ellie Smeal's press conference she gave yesterday. She told the press about the growing danger in the State Capitol. To reduce the danger, she and NOW have decided to remove all of their people. They are going back to the precincts where the campaign began. They want to apply pressure on the Governor and Speaker from the districts. So the ERA campaign is now out of the gallery and onto the streets. Ellie wants it to be clear to the press and to the people that NOW will not be partaking in anything illegal or threatening.

As of today, NOW will leave the guard around us in the rotunda. I hope she means that! I would be terrified to be there without them. Our band of eleven women is falling apart, to be sure. Four of us are in wheelchairs and the rest of us are wandering around in a daze. The keepers practically herd us to and from anywhere we have to go. Once in our places, we can sit and look hungry; we just need some bright and trustworthy energy around us.

After the meeting, J.R. and I went to a movie, *Author, Author*. It was okay. I just wanted to get back to my bed. I feel as if I could sleep forever. We sit in our rooms with the air vents blocked, the windows shut, the doors closed, under the covers and are still freezing. Dina finds it to be the worst part of this. She hates being cold. I remember Illinois being hot and sticky in the summer.

I think that the desire for food has been replaced entirely by wanting to be left alone. We all just want to be quiet and warm.

Sunday, June 20
Day 34

What a great day I had today. J.R. and I drove around all
day in Dixie's car in search of the Land of Lincoln. Just before
we left, I called my brother. He is going to have surgery on July
6, double hernia. I really like him. We are completely different
people but he makes room for me in his life. He disagrees with
most of my opinions but puts all that aside.

J.R. and I stopped at the hospital to see Mary Ann. She
looks awful. It is scary to see one of us in the hospital. Dina
and I have talked a lot about putting forward the intention
for all of us to stay well. We have refused to let in thoughts
of doctors, hospitals or illness. It is a big lesson here, about
leverage and honor, about press and privacy, about prayer and
politics. Is this oil and water? Can prayer move policy? I have
no idea.

We started our tour at Lincoln's Tomb. J.R. had not been
there on Memorial Day and she wanted to see it and take pictures.
The whole place is very impressive. The Great Liberator is well
remembered. J.R. rubbed the nose on the big statue for good luck. I
am not sure she actually reached it, but she tried. We drove around
the cemetery for a while. The Midwest trees are so beautiful. There
are hills and winding roads with graves sprinkled everywhere.

While driving through the cemetery, we spotted a lot of toys and stuffed animals just off the road. It was so intriguing that we parked to get a closer look at the graves. There were for children! Oh my god. Pinwheels and flowers. I cannot imagine losing a baby.

Then we went into Mr. Lincoln's home. It is a cute two story house with a white picket fence. I was so surprised to see his bedroom. My mother's guest room bed is the very same one. She had always called it the Lincoln bed, but I had no idea what she meant. The gift shop was fun. We bought salt and pepper shakers. There were satin pillows with paintings on them.

We went to a flea market at the Illinois fair grounds. I bought a bunch of gifts for people back home. I wanted to buy the blue Shirley Temple glasses, but I couldn't afford them.

We had to go back for the 6:00 P.M. business meeting. We totaled up the money people sent in and it came to over $11,000. Our expenses are running about $6,000: postage, printing, emergency room. We spent over $700 on bottled water. The idea is to split whatever is left after expenses to cover lost income and the travel home. Mary Ann has asked us to not make any final decisions until she gets information about her health insurance.

Ellie is very upset about the article in yesterday's State Journal Register. The headline reads, "NOW President disavows Militant Grassroots Group." She never intended that to be inferred by pulling her people out of the rotunda. She only wanted it to be really clear that if something did happen, it was not NOW.

I think that there is a big possibility of something happening if only because everyone expects it. Chances are good that someone may come along who wants to create an experience, get a bit of attention or just go berserk at the thought of men and women being equal. Ellie removing the Green & Whites is just her own form of active resistance. She removed her troops and prevented any confrontation.

Since we are going to the rotunda under any and all conditions, Ellie has recommended that we hire a bona fide legal observer. Monday we are going to have an official photographer with us to document everything.

This is getting complicated.
All I want to do is sit and fast and wait.

Monday, June 21

Day 35

To get up in the morning and put on my white clothes and purple sash has become an exhausting event. We all know it's over and yet we must play out the drama we've begun. As of yesterday it feels as if we are preparing for defeat. I remember around day five, we planned to stay for just a few days after the deadline to deprogram, eat wisely and adjust to the outcome. No one would even consider that now. Everyone just wants to go home.

Mary misses her kids. Dina needs to get back to her business. Woody, Sonia, Maureen, Shirley and Mary Ann are planning to be in Washington, D.C. for the rally on June 30th. It feels as if it's all beginning to fall apart at this point. Relationships are on the skids. There isn't a woman I talk to whose home life has stayed together through this ordeal. For that matter, I think we are all tired and lonely and hungry. I want to go home. Illinois votes tomorrow.

The morning ride to the rotunda is a meaningful metaphor. Eleven proud, powerful, courageous feminists moving and acting as one. If we were eating we would be enthusiastic and vibrant. We would be eleven women ready to go in eleven directions. Now we have folded in. It is a very big deal for anyone to have a special need because everyone has to be considered. Just going to the bathroom requires three people leaving the group. And it is the one thing we seem to need incessantly while drinking a gallon of water a day. Two eating women walk with one of us and guard the stall. This leaves two less guards with the others. Eleven strong-willed women, independent women sacrificing their strength for equality.

Today the rotunda was like no other. For weeks we had been stared at, trampled on, oogled over, pushed, shoved, and photographed. Today there was only us. The Capitol has been transformed from one huge political rally to a tomb. I don't see any Green & Whites. All this time we felt safe and loved by people wearing green and white. We have learned to be afraid of anyone in red and white. Now we've been told that some anti's are going to dress in green and white. I don't know who to trust now. I only know that we are in danger. The atmosphere in the Capitol has changed from chaos to razor sharp attention. Phyllis Schlafly has called for bodyguards and suspicions are growing.

And so entering that huge cold marble dome giving praise to the patriarchy was particularly gruesome today. There is simply no way to deny whose camp we are in, sitting, fasting and hoping. The only possible womanly thing in this Capitol is the statue in the center of the main floor dedicated to the Women of Illinois. What the Women of Illinois really need is the ERA. They need fair wages, full pensions, equal social security benefits and, moreover, legislators who vote in favor of humans -- not corporations.

Four folding chairs, three wheelchairs, a chain of body guards and us. What a tremendous crash from all of the heightened activity. And Illinois votes tomorrow.

J.R. went to the store and brought back a dozen copies of *People* magazine! We are all in it! WOW! E.T. is on the cover. I have to admit that I had hoped my mark in history would have been in *Ms.* magazine not *People*. I guess my face will be in dentist offices and barber shops all across the country. It is a darn good thing I broke down yesterday and told my mother where I am and what I am doing. My face was on the cover of

The Guardian, but my mother would never know about that. She was actually very nice and said that she hoped I did get the ERA. Somehow it always matters what she thinks. I would never change my behavior because of her, but I always want her approval. There is so little we agree on. I jokingly told her that my vote will always cancel out hers and that when she dies, I will finally have my vote count. Now it doesn't seem so funny.

We all loved the People article, especially the photos. But the article says that we are dressed by our aides. Oh really. I am walking on my own, even driving; I certainly dress myself. The only hard thing right now is coping. I just divide time by little increments and cope. If I can't smoke and I can't eat, then I will cope. It is the only thing I can really do now. What I miss the most is being alone. The only time I am alone is driving. I go to the post office to buy stamps or the drug store. God, I wish I could just be alone more.

At 11:30 A.M. a reporter came roaring through the rotunda shouting at us, "Florida has ratified! Florida has ratified!" The Florida House voted yes 60 to 58. How could this be possible? We were told it was going to ultimately fail and now this crumb has fallen at our feet. The press was all over us. They wanted to know our reaction.

At first I felt utterly betrayed. The patriarchy didn't even have the decency to fail it blatantly. I guess some legislators, seeking reelection, went pro-ERA at the last minute. I know it will eventually fail. And then I felt myself being swept away in hope. Could it be? Could our fast, the GGSCC's actions and the work of feminists for the last one hundred years have changed the course of history? Maybe sixty-one percent of the country had really gotten through to the legislators. Maybe the simple truth of the Equal Rights Amendment was irresistible. We screamed. We laughed. We cried. We hoped. And Illinois votes tomorrow.

The Hungry Heart

All my selves began lining up to state their position. My child wanted the ERA, pure and simple. My satyagrahi was sure that the fast had turned their hearts. My adult felt that this was only right, of course the ERA will pass. Then my feminist grabbed center stage and shouted, "No way, they aren't going to voluntarily relinquish their elite privilege. Never!" My woman sat in total defeat knowing all too well that this was just one more move on their chess board and all women are powerless until they find their own power source from within.

Reality began to set in. We all knew that this was one fleeting hollow moment of happiness and now we must wait for the next step. The Florida State Senate was due to vote in the next few hours. All of us agreed that we did not want to be sitting here for the result. The press would descend on us and we want to be together, but in private. So we left at the stroke of 2 P.M., which has always been our commitment.

First, we wanted to stop at the hospital to get Kate and Shirley who are visiting Mary Ann. Most of us waited in the van in the parking lot. I was sitting in the front seat and searched for news up and down the radio dial. How could there be nothing on the radio? This is the most important vote since 1920 for more than half of the U.S. population and there is nothing on the radio. Finally, I settled on a piece of classical music. For those last ten minutes, we were silent, drinking in Beethoven.

Maureen went upstairs to Mary Ann. I can't believe that Mary Ann has not broken the fast. She has been in the hospital for four days and not eaten. She is an inspiration for all of us. Maureen, Kate and Shirley walked back to the van and told us that the Florida State Senate voted No on the ERA -- 22 to 16. It is over. Oh God, it is over. No crying, no second chances, no alternatives. It is over.

The ride back to the motel was an eternity. We had not prepared at all for this moment. There was no way of knowing how much it would hurt. My innocence died right then and there, never to be reclaimed. We quietly agreed to meet in Dixie's room in a half hour to discuss what we would do with the press.

We all silently wandered to our rooms. I changed my clothes and went to the desk for mail. I got two letters today; one from Jane Gold and one from Kim. Kim says that she wants the ERA for her birthday. She said that there have been dozens of press calls to the Magic Speller and her uncle died last week. I got two mailgrams. One is from The American Humanist Association and this one from a woman in Laguna Hills:

> I continue to be overwhelmed by your courage. I cannot put into words the gratitude I feel about your sacrifice for me, my daughters and granddaughters and thousands of others like me. Mary Ann's illness finally moved the Orange County media into print action again. I am stunned by the very high price that consciousness raising is demanding of you. I love you all and send my blessing.

We all met in Dixie's room and told the press that they would have to wait for our statement. The NOW security guard arrived after a while. We all hugged and cried. There was talk of a caravan to Oklahoma. I can't imagine why. It is over now. There is nothing more to do. All that is left now is a formal press conference. Everyone needs it for closure.

We are fasting for the ERA.
The ERA is lost and so am I.

Everyone else is telling us that we cannot stop. We have to continue the fast because: 1) tomorrow the Catholics are coming, 2) it isn't entirely over until one more state goes down and 3) we should demonstrate our loyalty to the Pro-ERA women here in Illinois who are still working for ratification. And Illinois votes tomorrow.

We went outside and sat down on the grass. The press was waiting and poised. Dina said that she feels liberated. This has struck a fatal blow showing the absolute futility of working within the system. She says that she will never work within their system again. She is released. Sonia really took off, as only Sonia can. Without exception, she is the most moving speaker I have ever heard. The Spirit of Woman is glowing within her after being dim for weeks. She radiated saying that men hate women. Men devalue women. Only women value women. Women do the one thing that men cannot forgive them for, they grow middle aged. The women marry and take care of the home and children. The men throw them over for a younger, childless woman. They leave their children, marry a young wife and make some more. Divorced wives are left with no pensions, no social security and are the fastest growing group of people living below the poverty line.

Sonia went on to say. "We won't ever work in their system again. We won't ever vote for them again. We will vote for women who put women's agenda first. We will not forget who voted against women. Don't let Bush, Thompson, Ryan and Etheredge off the hook. Both parties care only about the corporate agenda."

The press was quiet. We were quiet. They wanted to know about the fast – so do I! We told them we are going to fast until it no longer serves our purposes to do so. We are fasting for justice, not just the ERA.

While this was all going on, the GGSCC broke their court injunction. Kris Griffith and Joyce Meyer, the two women who were injured by Representative Kelley, were with Mary Lee, Kari Alice and the entire group. They went to the Capitol and chained themselves to the Governor's office doors. After three hours, security showed up, cut their chains, carried them out of the office to the basement and let them go. When I heard that I just wanted to burst. I could never do what they have done. They are relentless dancers for Woman Fury. And oh, how furious She is today!

Judge Simon Friedman summoned them to a special session at 8 P.M. He set their hearing for Wednesday morning. He would then decide if he would hold them in contempt. That fool. He has no idea that he is just a figure in women's history, in human history, in the history of human liberation. It is his privilege to be in the presence of these great women of history. He is just a sniveling rat complaining that these women are a mere inconvenience.

Word has gotten to us that the Florida ERA workers are holding up. They stood inside of their Capitol and sang, "We'll never give up. We'll never give in." How well I know that song from the million verses sung in the Illinois rotunda. They were singing so loudly, they were heard in the House and Senate. Oh God, I hope they mean it. If November comes and they do forget who has voted against them, I think I will just die. My strident commitment is all I can hang on to right now. Success in November. Vote them out! Vote them out!

Representative Susan Catania, the sponsor of the ERA in the House, has released it to the press – the vote is TOMORROW. If Illinois goes down tomorrow, NOW will close down their campaign. If by some tragic mistake, Illinois does not ratify the Equal Rights Amendment and gender equality under the law is lost for the rest of the Twentieth Century, July will be a debacle. Everyone will rise up in anger. The nation will erupt in outrage. We will never be the same people. Inequality will be the law of the land and no will put up with it.

All we have to do is wait. One by one, women come to the movement as they experience discrimination first hand. In time every woman wakes up. Maybe the failure of the ERA will speed up the process. Maybe if millions see it, it won't hurt so much. And, if the ERA fails, they will see it clearly. I am so radicalized now. I'll never be the same. Where will I ever fit now?

And Illinois votes tomorrow.

Tuesday, June 22
Day 36

I have eaten. I have peanut butter breath. It is after midnight and I have eaten fruit compote, yogurt, peanut butter and diet 7up. I may not brush my teeth tonight just on the sheer chance that the taste will last all night.

It seems like a year ago, but it was only this morning that we began the day with a press conference for the Catholics. It was a sham and the press saw right through it. We had not eaten anything for 36 days and these self-important members of the Catholic clergy show up on the day of the vote to fast with us for a couple of hours. This is the first time I have felt that we are doing something insincere. The press clearly thought it was ludicrous.

In the rotunda, chairs had been set for them to sit with us. I tried to distance myself. I was cold and unimpressed. I worked on a crossword puzzle. The bishop and Jesuit showed up in cassocks which I know are totally optional. It is just grandstanding. The whole event lasted all of thirty minutes and left us surrounded with empty chairs.

Later in the morning, we went to the gallery, hoping the vote would be called early and we could get on with the day. It was a relief to get out of the rotunda. The Red & Whites are really aggressive and tension is high. With no Green & Whites, the landscape is only unfriendly and hostile. The Catholics were sitting in the gallery. The Jesuit was chewing gum! It almost knocked me out of my seat. Who do these people think they are? Who do they think we are? Why are they here disregarding true sacrifice. They would have done better to send a donation, push our wheelchairs or speak about the sacred history of fasting.

So there we all sat for over two hours watching our lawmakers at work. They knew we were there and they just proceeded as if it was just another day. Their desks are covered with food: Fritos, sandwiches, cokes, donuts and lots of red and white flowers. And if they needed more food, they would summon a page to fetch it for them. Do they realize that women all over the country are hungry for equality? Do they realize that women are waiting for them to vote for the Equal Rights Amendment? Could they be so self-absorbed and callous to the moment in history that faces them?

There must be thousands of people who sit nervously through legislative sessions waiting to hear their fate. They lobby and hope for a tax cut or funding. All the while the legislators sit in their big leather reclining chairs and make phone calls. It is shocking. What shocks me the most is that they are not embarrassed.

We finally agreed to leave and go back to the motel. Around 5 P.M. it came over the radio. Just before the vote, Monica Faith Stewart, Representative from Chicago spoke:

Thank you Mr. Speaker, Members of the House,
One hundred years before I was born, Sojourner Truth stood before a convention in New York City to speak on behalf of women's rights. She recognized the irony of this situation because she was speaking for colored women who, she said, had been thrown down so low that nobody ever

thought we'd get up again, but we've been down trodden long enough; we will come up again and so I am here. Thus, ladies and gentlemen, here it is one hundred and thirty years later that I am in this House and I rise on behalf of Black American women who are the descendents of slaves. I rise with Sojourner Truth, Harriet Tubman, Sally Hemmings, for Marie Stewart, for Zora Neale Hurston, for Fanny Lou Hammer, for Flo Clemmens, for these and hundreds and thousands of nameless faceless women that most of you who are in this white male-dominated, privileged chamber have never recognized and certainly won't remember.

I rise on behalf of women of color who have always had to fight for some modicum of self respect; I rise on behalf of Hispanic women, who don't have a voice in the chamber; I rise on behalf of Native American women who don't have a voice in this chamber; I rise on behalf of women who have never, ever been part of this protected class that some of the opponents speak so eloquently about, because I, ladies and gentlemen, am the product of slavery. I represent something that most of you have never had to respect, namely the color of my skin and my gender. But, I don't stand here to petition your "yes" vote, because what is your constitution to me? The Declaration of Independence was drafted by Thomas Jefferson, a man who, yes, was a Founding Father; who, yes, was a great statesman; but, yes, he was a slave holder and, yes, for thirty-seven years, he went into the bed of his slave, who he thought was the perfect woman. Why? Because she was a slave. And no, gentlemen, what is your constitution to me?

I don't come here begging for your "yes" vote, because those of us who are the lowest of the low find it very easy to accept that the men of this chamber would deny women equal rights. For they would seek, that same tradition would seek, to deny me culture, it would seek to deny me intelligence, it would seek to deny me beauty, it seeks to deny me humanity, and I say – quite frankly – what I would like to say to you I can't say. But enough is enough. I could give less than a damn what you think about me, my femininity, my humanity, my culture, my intelligence because it is!

So I stand only to present a truth and that is you can't vote this amendment up or down – quite frankly – it doesn't make any difference to me. I think that you are acting as people of your class and tradition have always acted, and you know what? It won't matter because we have survived much worse than this. Back when I was in school, we had a

saying, that if things didn't go the way you'd like them in the classroom, we'd meet you outside at 3:15. And so, white males of the world, it is now 3:15. I represent the majority of people on the planet, who are people of color and you cannot have your sovereignty any longer.
Why?
Because I say so!
Thank you.

And then came the vote. 103 for the ERA and 72 against the ERA. It was four short of the three-fifths majority required for an amendment to the U.S. Constitution according to Illinois House rules. What are we supposed to do? What are we supposed to feel? It is over.

The ERA is lost and so am I.

Unwillingly, I went to the First Presbyterian Chapel. I have had more than enough of male traditions, based on hierarchies and a male-faced god. But the good news is that Mary Lee called and she said that her group wanted to see us. Their trial was set for tomorrow morning.

What an event! I sat in the front row with Kathy, Vicki, Judy and Dina. It was grand, as grand as reform can be. The first speaker said, "If only you knew how beautiful you are." Vicki shouted back, "Oh we know!" It was so much fun. We needed to laugh and celebrate.

Mary Hunt, a feminist Catholic theologian spoke. She said that we are doing three things: 1) we are disturbing the peace, 2) we are in a patient revolution in which practice makes perfect and 3) we are a living prophecy. She said we are living today as if we had the ERA, thus making tomorrow today. Our gift is to live as if the ERA were law.

She spoke of the real historical significance of what we had done. Seneca Falls is now a landmark and there are plans in the works to make it a National Park. Someday Springfield would be remembered. Mothers will bring their daughters here to drive past the Ramada Inn and tell them about the fast. Slowly thirty-five people walked up the aisle one at a time and lit a small candle on the altar, one for each state that ratified the ERA. Then three women brought up three larger candles that were not lit. By the end, I was glad that I went to the chapel. It was a lovely funeral. It was a lovely birth.

A million hugs, a millions kisses and we were on the way. We drove straight to the IGA!. Seven famished women went crazy at the grocery store. We all came unglued at the baby food aisle. We careened around the store with two carts and it was no time for detachment. Yogurt, grape juice, cottage cheese, mounds of baby food. And the bill was over fifty dollars.

Peggy made Dr. Fulton's fruit compote for us. It was delicious. At this point, anything would be delicious. The motel room was giddy and silly and filled with joy. We laughed. We shrieked. We threw an Irish wake for the ERA.

I will sleep tonight.

I am an eater.

I am going home.

Wednesday, June 23
Day 37

It was a long day -- a grand day. I know I will never feel like this again.

Dina sprang out of bed at 7:30 and dug the room service menu out of the bottom of the top drawer. Dare we order food? What if the press gets wind of this? Well nothing could come of it because the papers won't run any story before the noon press conference. I ordered oatmeal, orange juice, poached eggs, wheat toast and coffee. The food arrived and Dina and I were sitting in the beds like two girls on their sixth birthdays. There was a knock on the door. It was too soon for room service to collect the trays. I asked who it was. Mary Barnes answered. I nervously told her that I would let her in if she promised to not scream. She agreed. Slowly I opened the door and she came in closing the door behind her. She saw the trays, shrieked and covered her mouth with both hands. I swear that never, as long as I live, will any meal be as much fun as that break-fast.

Some of us took off to court while others went to the hospital to re-enact last night's liturgy for Mary Ann. I was very relieved to be going to the hearing and not have to listen to the prayer service again.

The Hungry Heart

Our arrival at the courthouse was the most impressive moment of my life (so far). The press swarmed. They wanted to talk with the fasters about what we were going to do. We told them we are holding a press conference at noon. They asked what we thought of the Grassroots Group of Second Class Citizens. We told them that we are all determined women dedicated to equality. We admire them and are proud to know them.

We stepped into the courtroom and sat down. Judge Simon Friedman proceeded as if it was just any day in court. There was a long line of attorneys looking serious and official, as if they were prosecuting felons. One by one they called the defendants to the stand.

Berenice Carroll, Ph.D. 1969 Political Science.
...acts of Civil Disobedience have a positive effect. Their sole purpose was to give courage and inspiration to women who have not participated. All that was done was non-violent direct action.

Mary Lee Sargent, teacher of 14 years, American and Women's History.
Have you previously done Civil Disobedience?
No, regrettably, I have not. I came here to be persistent, a consistent aggravator to promote the ERA. We wanted to do things that were effective and essential. There was less than 200 hours left and we had to forgo the injunction.
Do you feel that this commitment to the cause is greater than to the law?
YES!

Joyce Meyer, (on crutches) TV monitor for the National Organization of TV Violence.
As Martin Luther King Jr. said, 'I cannot lend myself to an evil system.'

Kari Alice Lynn, 5 years as a house cleaner, 9th grade education and one year of college, survivor of rape and incest.

The Hungry Heart

Adalaid Balaban, co-owner of Balaban's restaurant, St. Louis. She was not one of the originals. She told her family that she simply had to go and see these women. Upon arrival, she realized that she had to stay.

The Prosecutor,
These women didn't come here to make women equal. These women came here to break laws. They were wrong when they thought they were being oppressed by a brutal system. They came to the Capitol angry, hostile and with a chip on their shoulders. I came here to suggest a sentence of 1-7 years, but now I believe that there is no assurance of compliance to the law and recommend 2-7 years.

The Defender,
This group of women has spent 10 years working toward the passage of the most important thing in their lives. They have tried everything possible, and with 200 hours left, they were compelled to break the court injunction and reenter the Capitol. If they were driven to this measure it is because of their zeal and exuberance. This movement has been set back dramatically. The court is faced with having to balance and consider good deeds, their commitment, their desperation and 10 years of work. I believe that the court should show mercy.

Judge Friedman,
This case is not about the ERA. It is not political. It takes no position on the amendment. I am wearing a robe of justice. It means 1) I must take the individual out of every day life and remind people of their responsibility and 2) I must remind the public that a judge is not acting as an ordinary person. I must uphold the injunction, otherwise we are going back to the jungle and neither of us want that. Even politicians have their rights and the court upholds those rights. The court does not object to their beliefs. But, it is the lack of discipline that creates criminals. This is the only way that this country can stand.

The Judge postponed sentencing until July 2. That way the injunction could stand and there is still a chance that the women might go, yet again, into the Capitol and thus further contribute to the case against them.

We dashed to the Capitol as quickly as possible. On the way to the press room, we were swept into a briefing by NOW. The Rules Committee has yet to meet. There is a sliver of a chance that they may vote on the rules change. None of us were buying it.

We went to the press room and met up with the others. Sonia stood at the podium and read our statement.

Wednesday, June 23, 1982
PRESS RELEASE
Women's Fast for Justice   Springfield, Illinois

Many of you have asked us if we would consider the fast successful if the ERA were not ratified before June 30.

Today we conclude 37 days of fasting; we announce that, yes, we do consider the fast a success.

We 7 women, representing millions of women across this country, have demonstrated that ordinary women can do extraordinary things and that women can be more than they dream they could be.

If nothing else, this message of courage that has gone out across this country has made this fast successful.

The fast has empowered and unified women and strengthened feelings of sisterhood.

Having succeeded in these ways we have invited you here to announce that our fast and this particular witness is at an end. We also invite you to witness the beginning of a new era - an era of women moving towards their own agenda and putting it first in their lives, their laws, their economics, their electoral politics and their spirituality.

Here's to the new era of women.

We toasted the press, the country and ourselves. Seven happy women stood spilling grape juice on their battle worn whites.

On the way to the motel we stopped at the Colonel's for chicken salad. We ate in the car with our fingers. J.R. and Dixie went to the Ramada dining room for lunch. I followed and tip-toed over the previously forbidden threshold. I stared at the brightly illustrated menu and looked over my shoulder at the salad bar. I excused myself, went back to my room and sobbed.

It is really over? Will I ever do anything as noble and pure again in my life? For over a month I taught myself that food and eating were the enemy of women's rights. All of the colors and varieties on everyone's plates were instruments of oppression. What have I done to myself?

J.R. came to my room and took me downtown to pick up the thank-you cards we ordered. They are really beautiful. We stopped at the photo lab and got her proof sheets. J.R. has documented everything. It will be alive in her pictures. Then we went to the mall. I ate a 15 cent chocolate chip cookie. It was very small and lousy. We squeezed into a photo booth and laughed like fools. Then we went to the Dairy Queen and I ate a child's hot fudge sundae.

Most of my stuff is already packed. All of us are leaving tomorrow except for Dixie and Mary Ann. They will leave when Mary Ann's health permits.

There was a small party at the NOW countdown campaign office. Sonia was so funny -- she pulled her chair right up to the buffet table and ate jalapeno dip. Everyone sang and held hands. We all know that what we shared here is rare and permanently part of who we are. Tomorrow we will go home to people who love us but they will never understand. This event belongs to us and that can never change. We met our fears with courage, embraced our weakness with togetherness and marched toward truth.

> Mary Jane stood on a chair and said a few things;
> The Governor said that since Memorial Day, he has only gotten fifteen thousand pieces of pro-ERA mail. He clearly lied as the NOW message brigade alone sent over three hundred thousand. The NOW phone banks ran consistently from 7:20 A.M. to 2:30 A.M. We did nothing wrong. We did everything right. Go home and tell everyone of the work that was done here.

Back at the motel I could think of only one thing -- the candy machine. I went and bought a Three Musketeers Bar. I began organizing my things and finished around 1:00 A.M. I ate a third of the candy bar and stopped, thinking it might kill me. I wrote out my thank-you cards so they would have a Springfield postmark.

Springfield, Illinois

THE HUMAN SPIRIT,
when united for the cause of Women's Liberation,
empowers, strengthens and makes the impossible possible. Your loving contribution has sustained us in this effort and brought you to our side to stand with us while fasting on behalf of women.
Please accept our deep gratitude and appreciation.

THE SEVEN WOMEN FASTING FOR JUSTICE

Zoe Ann Ananda	Dina Bachelor
Mary Barnes	Mary Ann Beall
Maureen Fiedler	Sonia Johnson

Shirley Wallace

May – June   1982

It is 3 A.M. and I have written forty-three cards. I hope I didn't forget anyone.

Dear J. R.,

You gave me laughter when I only wanted to cry. You gave me family when I felt alone. I await the privilege to repay you. I only hope I am equal to the task.

Dear Judy Block,

Your dark beautiful eyes, so full of knowing and loving glances, I will carry them with me always. You gave me safety when I was most vulnerable in my entire life. That is true love – true care. My wish for you is that you are cared for when life asks you to sacrifice your brave independence. My wish for me is that I might be one of the women who safeguards you. It will be my privilege.

Dear Kathy Samer,

This is impossible – we have already said so much with our eyes – our pausing to watch as the other passes – hands resting on shoulders. Sisterhood was just a word until I came to Springfield. We are kin and I am proud to be your sister. Thank you, Kathy, for everything you gave me, seen and unseen, heard and unheard, but always felt.

Dear Vicki Fuergeson,
I'll never go to church again without you! I certainly enjoyed
your sweet company. You have found a way to make loneliness
impossible – what a gift!

Dear Mary Lee and Kari Alice,
My sincerest hope is that I have expressed to you both how
deeply I love you. I will write again when I have a better
understanding of what happened to the 3 of us in June 1982
– to me. For now all I can possibly say is that I see your glorious
faces and see history – women in history. And then when I
look deeper – you make me feel that I am part of that history
too.
We have felt what only a few will – I am sorry to say.

It is 4:45 A.M. My room is so quiet. Dina is whereabouts
unknown. I have seven white roses on the table and all of my
stuff in boxes and suitcases. I am excited about going home.
The alarm is set for 6:30. Oh boy, one hour and forty-five
minutes of sleep. In fact, I feel so alive I don't think I will be
able to sleep at all. I feel like chirping like one of the birds I
have heard out in the corn field behind the motel.

I can't believe it is over.
Who will I be when I get home?
I am just Zoe after all.

Thursday, June 24

Our plane has finally taken off and for a moment there, I thought they would not let us on board. The airlines instantly recognized us and were aware of our circumstances. Dina and I have on our whites for the airport reception in Orange County. Our faces are on the front page of every newspaper and I guess we look worse than I imagined. They said that they don't want to take on any health risks. They relented when we told them that we are under a doctor's care and that a doctor was meeting us at our destination.

I must look even worse because I only slept for twenty minutes last night. Dina got back to the room around 6:45 A.M. and breakfast was set for 7:00 A.M. We invited the press and anyone else who wanted to come. People were just roaming in and out of the Ramada dining room. Oatmeal and toast was all I could handle. I think the lack of sleep and the wicked food I ate yesterday may be building an intestinal bomb.

Sonia, Maureen and Mary left for a 9:40 A.M. flight to Washington D.C. The good-bye was anti-climactic; just some simple words in the parking lot.

It was only 9:00 A.M. and time was slithering on. The miserable feelings I got when I first quit smoking are surfacing again. I am pulling on my hair and breathing is becoming more and more shallow. Rich Woods came by to bring me a box, tape and some Rolaids. Eating just isn't fun. It isn't social. It is an act of filling one's self. My body is so dormant that my stool looks practically unprocessed. In an effort to calm down I went outside and lay down on the grass. I gave myself entirely to Mother Earth and asked her to center me, to ground me. I paused and listened to the planets vibrate in and through me. It really helped.

Today is my sister Mimi's birthday. She is forty-six. I wish I had gotten a present off to her. She bought *People* magazine and saw me on the national news. I thought to call her but I can't seem to concentrate.

Dixie jogged by after settling the motel bill. It was $8,600 and is being paid entirely by NOW. It seems like a huge amount of money to me, but actually it isn't a fig in a multi-million dollar campaign.

We made a quick visit to the hospital to say goodbye to Mary Ann. She looked so weak. She is so infinitely patient, so long-suffering, so Quaker.

Dina and I were insistent on buying some plain yogurt so we stopped at a grocery store. Even though we were both in pain from what we had eaten the day before, we have no idea what food will be available in the next several hours and need this limited control in what we eat.

The airport was a vision of green and white. Judy, Vicki, Sandy, Louise and Kathy were all there to surprise us. We kissed and hugged and cried and laughed. Judy has beautiful eyes. Vicki's smile can light up a night sky. Kathy stands so tall and proud. I guess I am really going on and on here, but I am afraid that I will forget something and I want to remember every detail.

We walk a few paces, they wave and cry.

I go out the door, turn and we all wave.

On the plane, one glance back – they are waving.

And to my delight, they stand on the runway edge waving goodbye ceaselessly. And I, high above the clouds, with sweet innocence wave out my little window until I am well out of sight.

I miss them already.

Afterword

Upon my return to Newport Beach, The Magic Speller, my poodle and my lover, my life fell apart entirely. While in Illinois, I thought that I would be returning to a loving home, a quiet time and a slow return to work. None of that became the fact.

While I was in Springfield, Maria had made plans for a new life with someone else. I had no idea. It was a devastating blow. Certainly it was fortunate that I did not know during the fast. But many women risked and lost relationships while working for the ERA -- I was just one more.

In regards to fasting, you might find it interesting that for many months, I wanted to eat only white things. I ate cottage cheese, plain yogurt, plain baked potatoes, white toast and oatmeal. I think it was about limiting the colors and textures on my plate. Anything more was nauseating. Actually I found it hard to open cans of dog and cat food as they looked and smelled awful. Other than that, eating again was not a problem. The only thing I truly hated was that people who did not know about the fast would tell me how great I looked. They would ask if I had been to a spa or weight camp. Yes, I had lost weight, but not for vanity or dieting. I steadily and readily gained it back, as eating was eminent.

The Hungry Heart

It seemed as if the Women's Movement fell apart too. When no one lost an election in November because they voted against the ERA, the whole thing was just too much. The local NOW chapter began to fade. I put together a lecture with slides about Springfield and could not create any interest. I think it was all too painful. No one wanted to hear about it. They just wanted to put it in the past.

But the truth is that I learned so much that even twenty-two years later I draw on it often. The fast was a total transformation for me, inside and out. I learned that all human beings are on a path of transforming adventures that unfold right under our feet. Whenever a person says yes, life delivers lessons both timely and appropriate. It is unavoidable and the best thing to do is step lively and surely.

Just a few months ago I met a twenty year old man who was standing on a picket line outside of a grocery store. I asked how it was going and if management was budging. He told me that he didn't know and he wondered if the strike was working at all. I told him that it really doesn't matter. What really matters is that this strike will change him. He will know for the rest of his life that he can choose the hard road if it is the right road. He will know that he can get by on less, maybe risk the immediate future, and survive. He will know for the rest of his life, what it is to stand and demonstrate his beliefs. He is changed forever. That is the true significance of the strike for him.

M. K. Gandhi took the high road, the hard road, often on foot. He never stayed home because the fight was un-winnable. He began his experiment with truth in 1907 in South Africa. His final campaign was working and fasting for peace between the Hindus and Muslims in the late 1940's.

Even though apartheid continued and the Pakistan/ India conflict rages on, Gandhi was ultimately and utterly victorious. He did not measure his success on the social or political results. He knew and verified that the search for truth is a solitary journey. He used his body to do his research and his soul was irrevocably transformed.

Now we can see how significantly he influenced thousands of people he never knew or imagined. Martin Luther King Jr. and Nelson Mandela and countless marchers, demonstrators, men and women have come to see that Gandhi's legacy is not the social outcome of his causes, but his personal dedication to truth. He stood squarely at the fork in the road, made an assessment and put one foot in front of the other.

Evaluation was concurrent with the action. As the age old question is answered; the end is the means, the means are the end. None can be unwoven. I cannot be violent to create non-violence. I cannot wage war to end war. I cannot lie to establish honesty.

And so I chose my beachhead -- legislative equality for genders, Springfield, Illinois, 1982. In that particular battle my body and mind were often adrift, but my soul was grounded firmly in my ideal. I placed my feet squarely, embraced the conflict, wrestled with the issues and trusted my spirit. I believe that my spirit sent me there and could not fail. It did not fail.

I have often been told that I am an idealist. While the accuser is admonishing and cautioning me, I always say, "Thank you. There is no one I would rather be." For 37 days I put my body on a shelf and let my spirit have her way unfettered. I trust her and she has told me that the very best a human being can do is to give form to their ideals.

The Hungry Heart

I have learned that if you have an ideal you believe in, test it with your life. Take your stand and give it form. It is your vision and you are responsible for it. No one else is going to come along and pave your road. The very fact that the vision occurred to you makes it yours. If someone else was meant to do it, the vision would have come to them. If you believe in social equality, live it. If you believe in non-violence, remove violence from your life. If you believe in kindness, first you must be kind to yourself.

You must go first.
You are your laboratory,
this is your experiment,
you are your result.

Zoe Ann Nicholson
Newport Beach, CA.
August, 2004

Lune Soleil Press
Order Form

Internet	www.lunesoleilpress.com
Phone	866 298-1080
FAX	949 642-8560
Mail Order	Lune Soleil Press
	3419 Via Lido, Suite 614
	Newport Beach, CA 92663

_____ **The Hungry Heart**
(quantity)   *($21.95 each)*

_____ **The Passionate Heart**
(quantity)   *($21.95 each)*

_____ **Matri**, Letters from the Mother
(quantity)   *($8.95 each)*

add 7.75% if mailed within California
shipping: $2.00 standard or $5.00 priority

Payment options:
☐ Check
☐ Credit Card   ☐ Visa   ☐ MasterCard
Name on
Card _____
Card Number _____
Exp.date_____

Shipping Information
Name _____
Address _____
_____
City_____ State _____ Zip _____